Psychotherapy
Lives
Intersecting

Psychotherapy
Lives
Intersecting

Louis Breger

Transaction Publishers
New Brunswick (U.S.A.) and London (U.K.)

Library of Congress Catalog Number: 2011014055
ISBN: 978-1-4128-4575-5
Printed in the United States of America

Library of Congress Cataloging-in-Publication Data

Breger, Louis, 1935-
    Psychotherapy : lives intersecting / Louis Breger.
        p. cm.
    Includes bibliographical references and index.
    ISBN 978-1-4128-4575-5 (alk. paper)
    1. Psychotherapy—Biography. 2. Psychotherapist and patient—Biography. I. Title.
    [DNLM: 1. Psychoanalytic Therapy—Autobiography. 2. Professional-Patient Relations—Autobiography. 3. Treatment Outcome—Autobiography. WZ 100]
    RC475.B74 2011
    616.89'14092—dc23
    [B]
                        2011014055

Dedicated to the Guys: Eugene, Dan, Sandy, Robert, Dave, and the Sunnyside Boys—Skin, Bill, Art, Les, and Toad.

Books by Louis Breger

Clinical Cognitive Psychology: Models and Integrations (1969)

The Effect of Stress on Dreams (with I. Hunter and R. W. Lane) (1971)

From Instinct to Identity: The Development of Personality (1974; reissued 2009)

Freud's Unfinished Journey: Conventional and Critical Perspectives in Psychoanalytic Theory (1981)

Dostoevsky: The Author as Psychoanalyst (1989; reissued 2009)

Freud: Darkness in the Midst of Vision (2000)

A Dream of Undying Fame: How Freud Betrayed His Mentor and Invented Psychoanalysis (2009)

Contents

Prologue

*Throughout the therapy experience with you, I always felt like a person in a relationship, rather than a specimen to be understood by you, and then explained back to me...you communicated an utter lack of judgment, an acceptance of the aspects of my life about which I was the most embarrassed, and modeled that **Not Knowing** was okay.*
—Elizabeth

This book is aimed at all those people who are considering treatment for their psychological and emotional difficulties. It should also be of interest to therapists from a variety of backgrounds, as well as students in the field. For a great many people, psychotherapy continues to be associated with Freud and the version of psychoanalysis he created. Endless cartoons depict a patient—who may be human, dog, or cat—lying on a couch with a bearded analyst sitting behind taking notes. This version of psychoanalysis lives on, despite the fact that a great number of contemporary analytic therapists do not practice in this way. Typically, when major changes occur in science, social science, or the humanities, they percolate down to the general population within a reasonable period of time. This has happened very little with psychoanalysis. People who are considering analytic psychotherapy today should know that there are strikingly new versions of treatment in which patients do not lie on a couch with a silent analyst sitting out of sight, telling them their troubles can be traced to their childhood sexual fantasies: where the doctor is the expert who "knows"—who has access to the secrets of the unconscious—which he interprets to the patient, who is pushed to accept this "wisdom."[1]

This book explores contemporary analytic psychotherapy in its full complexity, drawing on the responses of many of the patients I have seen over the last fifty years as they describe, in their own words, what was helpful and not helpful in our work together. Since many of these responses were collected many years after the conclusion of their therapies, they constitute a long-term follow-up which will reveal whether the changes reported at the end of the therapy lasted over the years. These accounts will be presented by the patients themselves as opposed to the typical account written by the therapist or psychoanalyst. While their identities will be disguised for reasons of confidentiality, they are, in fact, the coauthors of this book.

I will also present a certain amount of autobiographical material. Since I have been mainly retired for the last few years, it has given me time to reflect and look back over the many years I have practiced psychotherapy. As I wondered about all the patients I had seen, the idea occurred to me of contacting them and hearing what they had to say about our work together, in a number of cases many years earlier. It was also an opportunity to look at myself and see how my own background influenced the particular kind of therapist I became. While it has been a rule in Freudian treatment that analysts reveal nothing about themselves, even within modern approaches, it is relatively rare for the therapist to speak about his or her own life in any detail. In other words, while there is a great stress on the *relationship*, and some contemporary analysts describe their emotional or "countertransference" reactions to patients, they still do not reveal very much about their own lives.[2] This is a complicated matter, of course, since knowing about one's therapist may or may not be helpful. While I think the Freudian rules of "anonymity" and "neutrality" are almost always useless, if not harmful, it is still not clear how much knowledge about the therapist's life *is* helpful. So, while I will include a certain amount of autobiographical information in this book, I leave important material out to protect the privacy of my children and because it would not necessarily be helpful to patients should they read it. I have found that patients typically do not want to know that much about me early in their therapy but, as the years progress, many of them find such information important.

1

Against Dogma

There are three forces, only three, on this earth that can overcome and capture once and for all the conscience of these feeble, undisciplined creatures, so as to give them happiness. These forces are miracle, mystery, and authority.
— Feodor Dostoevsky, *The Brothers Karamazov*

In his brilliant *Grand Inquisitor* episode in *The Brothers Karamazov*, Dostoevsky depicts the need many people have for powerful authorities and charismatic leaders, along with belief systems—religions, political ideologies—that offer answers and certainty; which prescribe a way of life in absolute terms. Societies do need leaders and belief systems, of course, but these may be flexible or rigid, adaptable or obdurate, democratic or authoritarian, benign or punitive. And, what is necessary in one sphere may be inappropriate in another. An army at war may require leaders whose decisions cannot be questioned, but the methods of a general or drill sergeant are ill-suited to the raising of children. So too with psychotherapy and the many ways that people seek help for their psychological distress. Therapeutic practice should be flexible, open-minded, and nondogmatic, but, all too often, the field has been dominated by powerful leaders and their orthodox doctrines.[1]

You feel unhappy, sad, depressed, suicidal; overburdened with shame, self-loathing, or unfathomable guilt; little things frighten you to the point of phobic anxiety; you cannot seem to find a satisfying or loving relationship and each person you become involved with turns out to be a replica of the hostile, abusive, or sick man or woman you were with previously. You drown your sorrows in booze, drugs, or food, which then become problems themselves as you struggle with alcoholism, addiction, or obesity. You are stressed out, terrified, enraged, traumatized, out of control, feel too much or can't feel anything. What is a troubled soul to do?

There are so many treatment options today that finding the right one may seem an overwhelming task. You can turn on the TV, and Dr. Phil will tell you what is wrong and what to do about it. Your physician or a psychiatrist can prescribe one of the many mood-altering drugs. You can go to alcoholics anonymous, or one of its many offshoots—narcotics anonymous, over eaters anonymous, gamblers anonymous, sex addicts anonymous—or enter rehab, to deal with your addiction. Exercise may help with disruptive emotional states; you can take up marathon running, biking, tennis, golf, or put in long hours at the gym. One can turn to pastoral counselors, spirituality, and religions of many kinds.[2] From the East come practices such as Buddhism and many forms of meditation, as well as Yoga, Karate, and Tai Chi, all of which may calm anxiety, put one in a peaceful state, or give meaning where confusion reigned.[3] Or perhaps massage or Body Work is what is needed. Then there are marriage and couples therapists to help with troubled relationships, grief counselors to deal with painful losses, or, new on the scene, coaching. One can seek out friends for comfort, find shoulders to cry on. Or—and often as a last resort—you can see a shrink: try individual psychotherapy.

Again you are faced with myriad choices. What kind of therapist: psychiatrist, psychologist, social worker, marriage and family counselor? Freudian, Jungian, cognitive-behaviorist, existential-humanistic, eclectic, or some other? Since the 1960s the field has become crowded with such a range of practitioners that it is difficult to know what is best for your own situation. A brief course of cognitive-behavioral treatment to clear up symptoms or years of psychoanalysis? Perhaps, therapy is all a lot of bunk and your problems are due to faulty wiring of your brain, too much or not enough serotonin, and one of the new wonder drugs will clear things up.

There is a good deal of controversy over the effectiveness of psychiatric medications, which I will not review in detail here. While they seem essential in the treatment of a few conditions such as severe depression, bi-polar disorder, and certain anxiety states, there is also research that questions their effectiveness and suggests that at least some of their efficacy may be due to a placebo effect. Three recent books (Carlat 2010, Kirsch 2011, and Whitaker 2010) present strong criticisms of the ever growing use of such medications, largely due to the money and influence of drug companies. As one example, see Turner et al. (2008), who review seventy-four studies covering over 12,000 patients. They demonstrate how the FDA grossly inflates the positive effects of these drugs, claiming that over 90 percent of patients benefit when, in fact the number is about 50 percent, while simultaneously distorting or downplaying studies that show negative effects. In two highly critical articles, the distinguished physician Marcia Angell (2011, 2011a) lays out the arguments and evidence that demonstrates how psychiatric medications have been widely overused, largely due to the financing and influence of the pharmaceutical industry. She also points out the great expansion of psychiatric diagnoses, which then become the bases for increased drug use, especially troubling in children. For a balanced discussion, see Summers and Barber's (2010) chapter on psychopharmacology. They point out that there is an increasing use of medication in combination with psychotherapy though there is little hard evidence for the effectiveness of this to date. George Atwood (2011) presents strong arguments and case material for the damaging effects of antipsychotic medications in the treatment of schizophrenia and trauma survivors. As we will see, several of my patients found antidepressants, in combination with psychotherapy, helpful, though the drugs had little to do with the major changes in their lives, relationships, and views of themselves.

Each of these many approaches can be dogmatic or not, demand exclusive adherence or be open to collaboration with others. Some AA groups think psychotherapy is incompatible with their twelve-step programs, while others recommend a combination of the two; some psychotherapists believe AA dilutes and interferes with therapy while others will not treat alcoholics or addicts unless they are simultaneously in a twelve-step program. All of these treatments have their values and limitations; they may be useful for particular problems or work best with certain individuals. I know people who have received help from almost all of the approaches mentioned above and certainly do not think that therapy is the best solution for everyone. The focus here, however, will be on what I know best from my own experience: individual analytic psychotherapy.

Psychotherapy and psychoanalysis are themselves split into many schools and factions, typically named after a founder—Freudian, Jungian, Kleinian, Kohutian—with their own theories, terminology, journals, training programs, rules, and techniques.[4] And they each claim to be the best, a practice begun by Freud when he labeled psychoanalysis the "pure gold." Schools of therapy can offer answers, certainty, solutions, which is what some people crave, especially in times of trouble. And there is much of value to be found in a number of these approaches, but only if their ideas are used as starting points, hypotheses, hunches to be pursued or abandoned depending on the response of the patient. Any therapy becomes compromised when it hardens into dogma, when the same methods and interpretations are applied to everyone, when one size fits all. The type of psychotherapy I practice is the result of a long process of development that has taken me through university departments, a medical-psychiatric training center, psychoanalytic institutes, and a variety of research and scholarly projects. This journey has led me, I like to believe, to an approach that is neither miraculous, mysterious, nor authoritarian. There is some difficulty in knowing what to call the kind of therapy I practice. "Psychoanalysis" has too many connections to the old Freudian version while "psychotherapy" may be too broad. So I will call what I do contemporary or modern analytic psychotherapy, or, to be brief, analytic psychotherapy. What it actually consists of will become apparent from the case descriptions themselves.

An analyst some fifteen years older than me once said that, when he was beginning his training at the Southern California Psychoanalytic Institute in the 1950s, he sought out one of the senior members and asked whom he should choose as his training analyst. He was told to just pick anyone from the list of analysts approved by the American Psychoanalytic Association, the person did not matter since the technique and analysis would be the same. Freud had counseled that psychoanalysts behave like surgeons and, if you are having your appendix removed, any competent physician will do; his or her personality need not be a factor.[5] Contemporary analytic psychotherapy has come a long way from this idea now, and we currently talk about psychoanalysis as a "relational," "interpersonal," or "intersubjective" endeavor: a meeting of two people, each with their distinctive personalities and subjective worlds. Patients bring their history, symptoms, and life situation, and the therapist brings his or hers, including their specific training and clinical experiences. What transpires is a unique interaction of the two.

Over the course of fifty years I have evolved my own way of practicing analytic psychotherapy, and this book will illustrate what I have learned from my experience.[6] Psychoanalytic case histories—which, from Freud on, have been the primary evidence for both theory and technique—are almost always written by the analyst. It is quite rare to ask patients for their version of what transpired. In other words, most psychoanalytic cases are discussed solely from the analyst's point of view. As Stepansky puts it, "analysts have never incorporated patient reports into their comparative assessments of theory, technique and therapeutic efficacy" (2009, 163). Exceptions are Stoller (1973) and Yalom (1974) though the latter would not call himself a psychoanalyst. The work that is closest to the present study is the volume edited by Schachter (2005) which reports seven cases that were treated by seven different psychoanalysts. Each case begins with a lengthy account written by the analyst and in four cases the patients, after reading their analysts' accounts, wrote relatively brief versions of their experiences. Thus, that study differs in important ways from mine, which begins with the patients' own accounts, with them reading my versions later. While the analyses described in the Schachter book are, in general, more formal—four or more times a week, lying on the couch—they are more contemporary and relational than classical Freudian, in my view. In addition, there are suggestions that, while a great deal of interpretive work went on, what was helpful were the same factors that my patients describe. One patient in the Schachter study reported, "I'd say my analyst values...insight or at least highlights it more in our work...than I do. To me what stands out most over the course of time are moments of mutual intense feeling, moments where we both had a good laugh about something that happened or something that one of us said" (90). Another patient commented, "You and your analyst become sort of like a real friend like I never had before" (123). And a third said, "The fact that he becomes an active participant in each session has been most effective in the parts of my life that have needed help the most" (144).

Psychotherapy outcome research frequently uses follow-up reports by patients, though these are often checklists and not the kind of long personal accounts presented here. Most analytic psychotherapists do not read the psychotherapy research literature and psychoanalysts have, until quite recently, rarely done research on the effectiveness and outcome of their methods, the one early exception being the Menninger Project, summarized by Wallerstein (1986), which, interestingly, found that "supportive psychotherapy" was superior to psychoanalysis. For a comprehensive review of psychotherapy research see Roth and Fonagy (1996) and Shedler (2010). Hans Strupp and his colleagues have done a great deal of excellent research in this area, clearly summarized in his article of 1996. There is beginning to be some acknowledgment among psychoanalysts of the need for evidence for the effectiveness of their methods, as reflected in the reviews provided by Shedler

(2010), Summers and Barber (2010), and Curtis (2009). Of the various contemporary psychoanalytic schools, only the Control-Mastery approach was directly built from research findings (see Weiss 1993, and Silberschatz 2005).

While most previous work has been centered on analyst or therapist reports, I will turn this around and devote a great deal of attention to what my former patients have to say about their therapy. Among other things, I was curious to see how their lives had gone after the conclusion of our work together: whether the progress they made endured, regressed or expanded. I conducted an informal survey of over thirty of these patients, asking them to describe what they remembered as being most helpful/therapeutic/curative in our work together, adding that their answers could be as long or short as they wished, and assuring them that their identities would be disguised and confidentiality respected. I also asked them to report what was not helpful, what they remembered as nontherapeutic. The patient quotations used in this book are uncensored; I have edited out repetitions and extraneous material, changed some details to disguise patients' identities, but included the essence of their comments, whether these were positive or negative.

The way I use the responses of my former patients parallels my collaborative approach to therapy. After I wrote up each individual account—my memories of what occurred and theirs—I sent this material back to them so they could modify, add, or change what was written. Chapter 3 will demonstrate how significant growth in our mutual understanding arose from these continuing dialogues. In addition, rather than my choosing their pseudonyms, I asked each person to choose their own.

A few cautions at the outset. The survey is not strictly speaking scientific. The patients who responded to my questions were those who valued their therapy, while the few who did not respond were more likely to include those who were dissatisfied. In addition, this entire group of respondents, with a few exceptions, was drawn from the last thirty years of my practice when I was more experienced, more confident, and less likely to be defensive. Certainly, in the beginning, I made more mistakes and had my share of therapeutic failures, and the fact that they appear here infrequently is, in part, a function of the selective nature of the sample and the time it was collected. The issue of therapist–patient match is also significant. Clearly, cases in which patients came to see me and stayed in treatment for a long time were ones where both of us felt there was a good match. While I have been open to seeing almost anyone who was willing to give therapy a try, some people, from early on, did not feel I was the right kind of therapist for them and dropped out. So my sample of largely successful cases is made up of those in which both of us were relatively comfortable working together.

While contemporary psychoanalysis stresses the relational, interpersonal, and intersubjective nature of the enterprise, studies of therapy are still almost all confined to reports in which the therapist describes the patient and says little or nothing about himself or herself. Another innovative aspect of the current study is my inclusion of autobiographical material so the reader can get a sense of what kind of a person I am and how this affected the therapy. Finally, it is worth noting that, since many of the patients who responded to my questionnaire were seen more than twenty years ago, they constitute a long term follow-up.[7] This is very rare in the literature and will show how durable the effects of analytic psychotherapy can be.

2

Early Psychoanalytic Cases

I don't think I ever would have been sane enough to have children without the time I spent in analysis.

—Judith

I came to understand myself much better and accept me with all my foibles, quirks and faults. Not that I'm cured of them all, I just control them better and accept them as who I am without being so judgmental and hard on myself.

—Scott

I began doing psychotherapy in 1959 and, while a full-time professor for a number of years after that, continued to see patients, gradually increasing the number I worked with until I began formal psychoanalytic training some fifteen years later. In the earliest years, I was quite green and uncertain of what I was doing but, when I did see my first cases in full psychoanalysis, I already had a significant amount of clinical experience and felt more competent. But, let me go back to the beginning.

"Ralph" was a man I saw in 1959 when I was doing my predoctoral internship at The Langley Porter Institute in San Francisco. I was twenty-four years old and he was one of the first supervised cases assigned to me as part of my training. Being very inexperienced, my memory is that I was mostly silent—not knowing what else to do—and mainly listened as he described his difficulties as a first-year law student as well as his problems with various women he was involved with. I have very little memory of what else occurred in this therapy over fifty years ago. Ralph and I became friends some years later, and remain so to this day, and he has provided me with his version of what went on between us. He begins his account by describing his poor performance at law school and his troubles with a girlfriend. He felt he was about to have "a nervous breakdown" and came to Langley Porter where he was assigned to see me:

When I first met him, I was ambivalent about whether he could help me...he looked too youthful, he was about my age and looked very "square." I thought that he was too inexperienced to be of any help, he also looked very nervous and I even challenged him about his lack of experience and he anxiously mumbled something to the effect he thought "he could help me." [He is right; I was very young, square in the sense of being married with a child, and fairly anxious. The conventional side of my life may be what led me to focus on his not doing well in law school instead of other emotional issues.] *Being pretty naive and needing someone to talk to, I reluctantly accepted his help, often feeling that I was teaching him as much as he was helping me. Perhaps the most interesting helpful and positive elements of what went on in our work occurred as the academic year was coming to an end. Lou had focused a lot on my succeeding in law school since I had done well on mid-year exams without studying. I was hating school, more and more, and not keeping up with my classes. I clearly was being quite rebellious and not a very serious student.*

Having flunked out of law school, and after a few years of psycho-analysis, which I entered later, I began a Ph.D. program in psychology. Prior to leaving San Francisco, in the last session with Lou, he had tears in his eyes and said something like he had made a mistake by equating success in therapy with success in law school. He said by placing too much emphasis on my successfully completing the year of school, he neglected a number of important things in my life, and that he regretted doing that, especially concerning my feelings towards my father, who died suddenly toward the end of our therapy, and which coincided with my flunking out of law school. By neglecting this, I was denied the opportunity to work through my conflictual relationship with my father. In the last session, Lou was very choked up, teary, and seemed rather distressed. The next time I saw him was almost eight years later, in a different city, when we, purely by chance, encountered each other in a hospital room where we had both come to visit a man who was a former student of Lou's and a professor on my doctoral committee. When my professor asked how we knew each other, I was very surprised and rather anxious, but Lou rather spontaneously said I was "an old friend," and that was it. I was a bit dumfounded, very touched and pleased; it was a lesson in acceptance, equality, diplomacy, and humanity, a lesson, I never forgot, and, on a few occasions when I ran into a patient or former patient in a similar situation, I always evoke the Lou response: I'd say he or she is "an old friend." I also have on numerous occasions said to new patients, when cross-examined by them, that I felt I could "help them" and, on rare occasions, I have become teary and choked up with the emotions of a patient's experience and have, when appropriate, indicated that I may have made a mistake in focusing on some aspect of their life that wasn't as helpful as I had initially thought. The above reflect important therapeutic moments in my relationship with Lou, things that have played a role in my development as a person and professional, and certainly was a catalyst in our ongoing friendship that has lasted over these past memorable, but unmentionable, number of years!

Ralph's memories of our work together are certainly clearer than mine; I do not remember "tearing up," though I'm glad to hear that I was able to be so emotional. The admission of not being as helpful as I might have been does sound like me. Some of the things he mentions are examples of his modeling his behavior as a therapist after the way I had been with him, which is certainly a surprise to me since, at the time, I felt I was just groping about in the dark. We had no further contact after the conclusion of that one year of therapy, until our chance encounter eight years later. I cannot remember how but, since Ralph later became a professor of psychology and psychotherapist himself in the Washington, DC area, we got back in touch and became friends. Perhaps, some of his positive memories of what occurred in 1959 are colored by our later years of friendship.

The following three patients were seen during my training at a Psychoanalytic Institute in the late 1970s, almost twenty years after seeing Ralph. Because I discussed them with a supervisor during the first year of their analyses, and also because this was relatively early in my career, my work with them was more "Freudian" than that with patients I saw in later years.

"Judith" was a woman I saw for five years, four times per week, ending in 1980. She was in her early thirties: slim, intelligent, and working as a schoolteacher, a job that she felt did not provide a sufficient outlet for her creativity. She was quite anxious and guilty beneath her controlled exterior and suffered from a fear of fainting when going to the doctor, mild claustrophobia, and amenorrhea which prevented her from becoming pregnant though, at the beginning of her analysis, she said she was too fearful to become a mother. Throughout her childhood, her mother was over-involved with her older sister, who had a breakdown in high school from which she never recovered, spending the remainder of her life as a chronic schizophrenic.

I saw Judith once a week for a few months and then offered her the opportunity of psychoanalysis as a low-fee training case through the Institute's Clinic, which she was pleased to accept. Her sister's schizophrenia was a central issue in her life, which we spent much time exploring, since it seriously deprived her of her mother's time and love. Judith had become the family caretaker, with her needs and fears submerged, a pattern I have seen in other patients when sick or disturbed siblings take up an inordinate amount of parental time and interfere with their receiving the care and attention they need. They are typically forced to become premature adults, and this was certainly the case with her.

Judith was, in many ways, an ideal case in classical psychoanalytic terms. Her anxiety and other symptoms strongly motivated her involvement, yet were not so severe that they kept her from maintaining her marriage or working successfully. She formed a trusting and positive relationship with me, which went through various transformations over the course of the analysis. She lay on the couch, and a number of my interpretations were focused on the transference. Here are her thoughts about our time together, reported more than twenty-five years later:

> As a self-conscious person, I think that lying on the couch was essential to my feeling that I could open up and say whatever came into my head. I didn't have to see in your eyes or your face how you were reacting. At the time, I may have wanted you to say more in response to what I poured out, but in retrospect I think it was important that you let me blather on. When you did make comments, your insights were usually spot on. Go Lou!

> As for our relationship, I trusted you totally, though I always thought of you as an only slightly older dark and handsome man, so there was mucho attraction—and of course I believed you shared an attraction to me. That you never "crossed the line" was crucial to my continuing to work with you and to my trusting you.

[In response to my question about termination she said,]

> Only that I felt ready, proud to have gotten there, yet sad to leave you. Like a kid going off to college!

> I think of you very fondly. I feel I am lucky to have known you and I appreciate that we can be in touch as "grown ups" now...I don't think I ever would have been sane enough to have children without the time I spent in analysis. And I LOVED that you showed up at my book reading [Over twenty years after the end of her analysis, I went to a talk she gave about her latest book]... and that I didn't blow it even though I knew my SHRINK was in the audience!

The analysis was a great help to her; she became pregnant and that child is now grown, married, and working successfully; her second child is also doing well. Her marriage has endured and, about a year into the analysis, she switched careers and became a journalist. Her writing career expanded and continues to this day. Judith was not a deeply disturbed person and the more structured analytic process worked well for her. Her account—and remember this is many years later—indicates that lying on the couch and just talking freely was helpful and comfortable, and that my interpretations were "spot on." In my own recollections, I am not sure they were all so perfect; at the time I felt much more uncertain. She developed an erotic transference, which I interpreted, along with a number of other twists and turns in our interactions, some of which she may not remember. She also commented on several relationship factors: that I was, "honest, smart, calm, un-egotistical...and had a good sense of humor." Having had some contact with her in the last few years, it has been gratifying to see how happy and fulfilled she is, having close relationships with her grown children as well as satisfying, creative work.

The second case, "Scott," came to see me in his early thirties. I saw him for ten years, originally four times per week, and then tapering off to once a week, finishing in 1986. Attempting to work with him along the more usual psychoanalytic lines, as I originally did, was only minimally successful. He was referred by the supervisor I was seeing for my work with Judith, who told me, from his omniscient psychoanalytic position, that he did not think Scott was "analyzable" because he had a "sexual perversion," but I was welcome to try. The concept of "analyzability" is worth a brief comment since it bears on who—patient or analyst—sets the goals for the therapy. Patients typically seek treatment because they are in pain or psychological–emotional distress. Old style analysts present themselves as helpers—and the best ones often are, despite theoretical and technical impediments—but often there is a tacit agenda: to make the patient's unconscious conscious, to remove defenses, or to unravel the Oedipus complex.

Scott was a very driven and outwardly compliant man who grew up with an older, sick, depressed mother, and a father who, while nice enough, was never able to stand up to his wife or protect his son from her guilt-inducing attacks. He remarked early in the analysis that he did not think he had an Oedipus complex since his most striking memory of his mother was of her vomiting into the toilet. His childhood experiences with her left him feeling small, inadequate, quite anxious, and frightened of girls well into his college years. He compensated for his sense of guilt and inferiority by driving himself to study very hard in college, especially in his postgraduate program, and on his job working with disadvantaged children. In college, he married the first woman who was nice to him, but she turned out to be asexual, emotionally isolated, and unable to give him the love he craved. Nor was she, in Scott's eyes, a loving mother to their young son.[1]

For several years before he came to see me, he was caught up in a series of sexual affairs with women outside his marriage, fueled by a mixture of neediness and anger at women. He had one long-standing relationship with a woman, "Pati," whom he felt he really loved, but was also involved with four or five other women, and each of the affairs had to be kept secret, not only from his wife, but from each other. The whole complicated business had gotten out of hand; the more he was compelled—and it was indeed a compulsion—to see these women, the more frantic and guilty he felt. Consciously, he wanted to end the whole thing, divorce his wife, and be with Pati. Yet he felt he could not do this since it would mean leaving his son with a mother who he perceived as much like his own: condemning the boy to a life of terror and isolation as his childhood had been.

As a training case, I originally saw him four and five times a week on the couch and, following the advice of my supervisor, tried to get him to stop his womanizing, with no effect. The supervisor reasoned that, as long as Scott was "acting out"—dealing with his conflicts by actions in the world rather than experiencing the emotions and fantasies in the analysis—his unconscious conflicts would not be available, one of those psychoanalytic ideas that sounds good in theory but doesn't necessarily work in practice. When the required supervision came to an end, I could see that trying to get Scott to stop his affairs was a failure, and I was then able to change the way I worked with him. We agreed that he should sit face-to-face since, as we came to see, one of the main ways he had dealt with his fear and sense of inferiority, from childhood to the present, was by drifting off into fantasy, which he would frequently do when lying on the couch. We agreed that sitting up would be preferable; among other things, it would make it easier for him to stay awake during the sessions. Since, following my supervisor's advice and suggesting that he stop the affairs had only increased his guilt feelings, I told him that he would stop womanizing when he felt he was ready to do so. Both these changes, along with greater activity on my part, led to a more comfortable and open relationship. It took a number of years, but he gradually came to trust me and stopped the affairs on his own. He settled into a loving relationship with Pati and was finally able to divorce his wife, but not until his son left home for college. Neither a close relationship with me, years of analysis, or the many insights we worked on, would allow him to abandon this boy to a barren and depressing life like the one he had gone through as a child.

Once he was free of his first marriage and in one where there was mutual love and affection, the analysis wound down and came to an end. During the final sessions, he told me how, a short time earlier, he had sat up all night holding his aged mother's hand as she lay dying, an atonement for his anger at her, which further alleviated his sense of guilt. He was seeing me once a week by then, and we ended this ten-year analysis by mutual agreement. Here is his account, written more than twenty years later:

> *I have been thinking a fair amount about my time in therapy and have tried to encapsulate what it meant when all was said and done. I feel I received three or four major benefits from the experience: I was validated in my feelings about the situation of my marriage and was ultimately able to extract myself from it although it did not happen for a long time. I am not sure I would have been able to do it without the work of going through the process. Obviously I am very grateful to be able to spend the rest of my life with Pati and, other than I still work too hard, we are very happy together.*

> *The other main outcome was that I came to understand myself much better and accept me with all my foibles, quirks and faults. Not that I'm cured of them all, I just control them better and accept them as who I am without being so judgmental and hard on myself. I gained a lot of confidence because of that acceptance and feel a whole lot better for it.*

> *I came to have a much better appreciation for my parents even given their own unique problems and behaviors. I suppose it is inevitable that we come to think more of our parents at my stage of life but I seem to miss them more now than before and wish they had been around longer than they were so we could have got to know one another better. I did get to some sort of closure before she [his mother] died and I wish I could have with my dad as well. In any event I feel they did the best they could with what they had and I appreciate them more for it.*

> *In terms of the actual process and our relationship I guess I never totally bought into the Freudian thing and got more out of just talking about stuff as time went on. I don't think there were many*

'aha' moments in our sessions and more just gradual acceptance of what was really going on in my past and my life. It was a long slog but I think I finally got to a lot better place than from where I started. I was pretty comfortable with you as a therapist from the beginning as I recall and I eventually came to think of you as a friend and supporter. I think that is when I made the most progress. It helped that you shared stuff from your own life experience and it made me feel less intimidated in the relationship. 'Hey, this guy's got problems too.' The fact that you succeeded in your life problems didn't hurt either. I would have liked you to have been more directive at times and said 'Cut the crap and get on with it!' But that would not have been 'kosher' from the psychoanalytic point of view.

So this is probably too long and rambling but I just wanted you to know that I look back on my life now without much regret or guilt. I did the best I could with what I had and I'm in a pretty damn good place right now. I have a wonderful relationship with "A" [his son] and his family...Like I said Pati and I are great and are looking forward to more time together.

Remember how much we talked a lot about "The Catcher in the Rye" back in the day? I had forgotten all about that until recently. I'm winding down my career at "C" [the school where he works] and have given notice I'm stepping down as principal and just teaching. I guess the thing I feel best about was what I chose to do in life as a career and how lucky I was to "follow my bliss" as Joseph Campbell used to say. I have absolutely no regrets about what I have done now for almost forty years. It has been a hoot, as they say. It hit me a few months ago that I became exactly what I wanted to be, a catcher in the rye.

The third case was a man in his late twenties who I will call "Gregor," with thanks to Franz Kafka who, in stories like *The Metamorphosis*, gives an evocative account of the kind of suffering this patient endured. As Kafka put it in his story about a man in a sideshow who has made an art of fasting:

> *I couldn't find the food I liked. If I had found it, believe me, I should have made no fuss and stuffed myself like you or anyone else. These were his last words, but in his dimming eyes remained the firm though no longer proud persuasion that he was still continuing to fast. (The Hunger Artist)*

I saw Gregor four times a week for a year-and-a-half, ending in the late 1970s. He suffered from extreme anorexia/bulimia—quite rare in a man his age—sleep disturbance, fainting spells, and a variety of related symptoms. Until a year before coming to see me he had functioned at what he described as a high level: pursuing graduate studies, reading "all of Freud and Marx," and needing little sleep. This seemed to work because of what he called "eating and vomiting" and compulsive exercise, swimming up to three hours every day. Then the thought came to him, "I can't go on like this." The exercise stopped, and the vomiting, which was always done in secret, was discontinued. He sank into a terrible state and contemplated suicide. He saw two other psychiatrists, recommended by his father, who, he felt, gave him "bad advice" before coming to me for "a real psychoanalysis."

Gregor's disturbance cannot be understood apart from the family in which he was enmeshed. He described his surgeon father as a "thoughtless son-of-a-bitch" whose only interest in his son was as an extension of his own "over-blown ego." Several of my colleagues in the medical community, who knew the father, confirmed this picture, one calling him "the most narcissistic man I ever met." His mother had undergone treatment for cancer some years earlier and, while physically recovered, took to her bed and never left the house. She herself had suffered from anorexia when younger, would not prepare food, and required her son to shop and cook for her. The father prescribed a variety of medications—strong tranquilizers, muscle relaxants, appetite suppressants!—for both of them and they, in turn, took revenge on the great doctor by defeating his attempts to treat them. Unfortunately, their own bodies were the battlegrounds on which these self-destructive wars were fought. Gregor was certainly not "analyzable" or a likely candidate for psychotherapy, but my supervisor and I agreed that, since other treatments had failed, and he was interested in psychoanalysis, it was worth trying.

In my work with Gregor, I thought it was essential, above all else, that he come to trust me, to see that I was not trying to control him in any way, as his father did, nor enmesh him in my life, like his mother. So I was very patient, listened, and more than with any other patient, followed his lead. Since he knew a good deal about Freud and psychoanalysis from his reading, as trust gradually built, we could slowly begin to understand the complex meaning of his symptoms. They were complex indeed. "Eating and vomiting" expressed his emotions and conflicts in a concrete symbolism of the body: the need for good food and love, terror and rage at the lack of these, symbolic—and sometimes real—attacks on those who gave him "bad feeding," and a self-punishing guilt that tied his body in knots, led to terrible cramps, diarrhea, and fainting spells, not to mention the self-starvation.[2] There was also a belief system that he had put together from reading Freud's *Totem and Taboo* and the French psychoanalyst Lacan, in which eating was a "totem meal" in which he devoured "the father" and vomiting then "reestablished the maternal order."

The therapy sessions were largely filled with accounts of what he had eaten, his cramps, swollen stomach, how much he had shit or vomited, and whether he slept or suffered insomnia. It was as if he and I lived together in his gastrointestinal tract. While I tried to empathize with what he described, it was very difficult to be immersed in his extremely painful and bizarre world, and I struggled to stay interested and connected.

Gradually, he became more trusting, and even felt comfortable enough to show me some of the articles he had written in graduate school. But the growing strength of our relationship was accompanied by very disturbed reactions to my brief absences or vacations. During one separation he had a minor traffic accident and, another time, passed out in public. The end came when I received an angry, accusatory phone call from his father telling me that Gregor was dead. From later conversations with his one male friend, "Martin," I was able to put together what had happened. After a long bout of exercise, he lay down, drugged with a powerful tranquilizer supplied by his father, and apparently aspirated his own vomit in this stuporous condition and died.

Both parents made every attempt to cover up the death. His mother, in a brief phone conversation with me, said, "Maybe it's for the best." His father, whom I had spoken with several times on the phone earlier, made clear that he considered his son an embarrassment and seemed relieved to be rid of him. To the outside world, they pretended that Gregor never existed—there was no funeral, only immediate family members were notified—just as Gregor Samsa's family did in Kafka's *The Metamorphosis*.

I had a very complicated reaction to his death; he was the only one of my patients to die in all the years of my practice. I was quite sad at the loss of this young man, who was intelligent and trying to help himself as best he could. At the same time, it was not clear—given the extreme nature of his disturbance and his enmeshment in his family—if his death could have been prevented. Given my own propensity to feel guilty, I have to say that, while I felt very bad when I learned of his death, I was not aware of much guilt. Trying to treat him while he lived at home, where both parents undermined his attempts at an independent life, was extremely difficult, and he resisted my suggestions that he move out and room with his friend Martin. Nor would he or his parents consider hospitalization. In his mind, he needed to stay at home to "protect" his mother from his father's attacks. It is possible that another therapist could have been more helpful with him, but, in the end, I wondered if his death wasn't an escape from his impossible life situation. Since Gregor was clearly not a success in his analysis with me, his death might have led me to avoid such cases in the future. I do not think it did; I remained open to seeing anyone who was willing to give therapy a try. The case of "Nate," to be discussed later, shows successful work with a very disturbed young man.

Looking back on these early cases, it is clear that Judith got a great deal out of what was, in the main, a more traditional psychoanalysis. She found lying on the couch and free associating helpful, developed a number of transference reactions, which I interpreted, and the insights she obtained enabled her to change. She was the kind of patient who was able to benefit from this form of analysis, though there were a number of relationship factors at work as well. Scott was a completely different story. The supervisor who made the referral pronounced him "unanalysable," yet, by any standard, his analytic therapy was a great success. His own report minimizes the importance of interpretations and insights—as he put it, he "never bought into the Freudian thing"—and says he made the most progress when he felt I was "a friend and supporter," and valued my sharing events from my own life that helped him "feel less intimidated." And we made the most progress when we were sitting face-to-face. And Gregor's death was most distressing, though not surprising, given the near-psychotic nature of his disturbance, and how all attempts to separate him from his mother and father failed. Both Judith and Scott felt that interpretations and insights were important, though these were worked out collaboratively between us, tailored to them as individuals, rather then taken from theory. Both of them also pointed to relationship factors that, in the case of Scott—and Gregor too—were central. I do wonder if things might have gone more rapidly if I had seen these patients later in my career when I was more experienced. I certainly would not have wasted several years having Scott on the couch trying to free associate, and might have been more active with Judith.

3

Continuing Dialogues

The things that worked well for me in therapy were talking to someone who actually listened—frighteningly so, considering how much nonsense I talked about—and who was non-judgmental about that nonsense.

—Emily

In this chapter, I will discuss two cases where the patients and I had back and forth e-mail exchanges, following the initial write-ups. These dialogues led to important changes in our understanding, both of them as individuals and of the therapeutic process. I will first present my initial version, along with their first response to my questionnaire. This will be followed by the modifications they made after they read this material and, finally, a summary showing how these exchanges can be combined into more complete and valid accounts.

The first patient is a woman I will call "Emily"; she is described in an article I wrote on dream interpretation shortly after the conclusion of her analysis (Breger 1980). I saw her for five years, mainly three times a week, ending in 1979, with a few additional sessions in the 1980s. Her presenting problem was a self-destructive form of sexual activity. She had left her marriage to a seemingly nice and supportive husband for a series of affairs with men who, in her eyes, were disreputable in some way, and who ultimately disappointed her. In her dreams and fantasies she assumed a "masochistic" role vis-à-vis these "bad" men. The "masochism" was not extreme, she was never physically harmed, but just chose men who were only interested in sex rather than a meaningful relationship. This pattern was traced to what may have been a sexual molestation—or a sexualized relationship—with her grandfather, to whom she was very close as a little girl, but who also treated her harshly. He was the prototype for the scenarios she played out in her fantasies, dreams, and relationships, where she was a "slave-girl" to a "cruel master." We also did a good deal of work exploring her rivalry with her siblings, and what seemed like disappointment with both her mother and father, though these did not loom large in the analysis. As we will see, her own later reflections show this to be a very incomplete, if not biased, version of her childhood experience. Here is her own first account, written more than twenty-five years after the completion of the analysis.

When I think of all the time I spent "on the couch" and look at my life today, I have to start by saying thank you for whatever magic you worked during our time together. To quantify that magic is an interesting task...

Therapy gave me a foundation—a way of thinking about what I did and what I thought. Telling another person what you did, no matter how stupid, has an organizing effect on your thought process. When I was in therapy I tried to think of how to tell you some event. Thinking about something that happened with the intent of telling another person forces a type of thinking where, if you are conscious, you will see patterns and hopefully can catch yourself from repeating them.

The three things I think worked well for me in therapy were talking to someone who actually listened—frighteningly so, considering how much nonsense I talked about—and who was non-judgmental about that nonsense. I also thought that dream interpretation was very useful to me, even though it is cool these days to discredit it as so much foolishness. I particularly liked/still like remembering dreams and listening to my unconscious guide me that way. I like trying to see what there is to see in a particularly complex dream and use those thoughts to work through things, see where I am getting in my own way, or see things from another person's point of view. My dreams don't all have deep meaning, of course. Some of them seem to be a mundane filing of the day's events into some sort of order. Some dreams are prophetic or pay-attention-to-this types, like when I need dental work and I dream about my dentist. It is nice to have this tool at my disposal to help me along in life.

Dreams are useful, but I think the two most important aspects of therapy are being present-listening and non-judgmentalism. When one is in therapy, those are the gifts your therapist gives to you. If you are paying attention to the process and you grow and get well from it, those are the gifts you give others for the rest of your life. Trying to remember these things has been an important aspect of my life as a management consultant...a consultant serves well to listen and ask questions quietly to see what is keeping an executive up at night.

Helping him/her reach the issues and work out a plan has served me well in my work.

There are very few negatives that come to mind, but I guess the idea of transference is one thing I never related to. I always saw you as a real person and actually had trouble being angry "at" you as though you weren't there as Lou Breger. The idea of projecting feelings intended for another person onto you was something I never "got" during therapy. [She does not recall that, early in the analysis, she was outwardly compliant yet withheld her emotions from me, crying in her car after sessions but not with me. This paralleled her withholding herself emotionally from the men she was involved with.] *I remember best our second set of sessions in the 1980s when we sat across from one another and talked.*

What I wish had happened—although this is completely contradictory to listening and non-judgmental work—is that you had stopped me from my self-destructive behavior once in a while by being judgmental and pointing out to me what I was doing. I might have listened, but I wonder if I would have understood? I'll never know the answer to this one, but I feel I wasted a lot of time approaching life the same stupid way. A good crack on the head might have made me at least think about it.

Since Emily mentions our work with dreams as an important part of her analysis I will present a significant one that illustrates both her unconscious conflicts and the way we came to understand them.

I was living in a farming village and some Arab marauders came and bargained for twenty young women to take to their oasis in the desert. I'm one of the women: we are bathed, oiled and prepared for the trip across the desert on camelback. I enjoy this trek, feel strong, tough and able to withstand the hardship. We get to the oasis and are taken into an underground cavern or dungeon where we are placed in compartments around the side of a sort of cave. It feels cold and there is water dripping. The other women all seem complacent and happy, but I feel more and more suspicious. I don't trust them, it seems like there is going to be some kind of sacrifice—like the Aztecs used to do—of one or all of us. I feel threatened in a sexual way.

Her associations led to her anger at men and, eventually, we were able to relate the dream to the sexual surrender to "bad men" that she was playing out in her life, modeled on her early experience as "Granpop's little slave-girl." In the dream, she first draws strength from this, but then feels threatened. The specific reference to the Aztec sacrifice eventually led to the memory of a crucial early trauma in which, as a very small girl, she had a vivid memory of her mother having a bloody miscarriage at home. Granpop, who had lost his wife to uterine cancer, was panicked and, as he and an aunt scurried around, Emily sat in a corner, frightened and forgotten. The miscarriage was followed by the births of two siblings so that this traumatic, aborted pregnancy was followed by two normal ones and the births of her brother and sister. These new babies, close in age, caused important losses of her mother's time and attention. Her adult sexual pattern was, in part, an adaptation—a mastery—of the early trauma and these losses. If she did not have her mother's love, she would outdo her by becoming Granpop's special little girl.

By the end of her therapy, she had stopped the unsatisfying sexual relationships, moved from her job as a secretary to a successful new career and, some time later, settled into a marriage with "Peter," a gentle and loving man. She also gave a great deal of help to the troubled daughter that Peter brought from his previous marriage.

It is interesting that Emily's analysis set her on a path of self-exploration that she continued in the succeeding years. She still pays attention to her dreams and used what she learned in therapy in her work as a management consultant. So it is not surprising that reading what she and I initially wrote stimulated a host of additional memories and thoughts. Here is her second communication with me:

> I had considerable trouble writing my thoughts down. It was hard enough to organize my theories, but harder to deal with the emotional content of them. The idea has haunted me ever since you told me that I might have been molested as a child. I realized that much of my behavior during the period you knew me would indicate that might be so. The more books I read on the subject, the more I thought you might be right, but then—either out of denial or 'what-does-it-matter-anyway' or the fact that my career took off in a good way—I just put it in the back of the closet and let it sit. But once in a while I would find myself wondering why I couldn't remember something as traumatic as that. If I could remember my mother's miscarriage, why not that? It bothered me that it rang false, even though the evidence of my behavior might indicate otherwise. I concluded that my denial was due to my not knowing anything about psychology or children's reactions to trauma, acting out, etc. However, when I got your draft and the possible molestation was mentioned again, my discomfort with

the whole theory makes me need to explain different understandings that have come to me over the intervening years.

First of all, I am especially uncomfortable with the idea of my grandfather being an abuser. That does not fit with any of my memories of him. My grandfather was a mensch. He was an old fashioned, German disciplinarian, for sure, but he was also very loving and supportive of me when I was older. It just didn't fit that it would have been him. It violates my memory of him.

So, putting that diagnosis aside, I may be able to replace it with thirty more years of thoughts and observations, bits and pieces of evidence to the contrary, and the perspective that living out a life gives.

When I left my first husband, I felt guilty and insane. You said it yourself—"he was a seeming nice and supportive husband." But I will add today what I only understood unconsciously at the time of my analysis: that he was supportive only in so far as it supported his belief systems and his control over the events of our lives. He is still my friend and observing his life and his dealings with other women over the ensuing years has proven to me that I was right in leaving when I did. I would have been on drugs or going to AA meetings now if I had stayed.

I also have years of observing my siblings' behavior. Today my brother and sister both are severe Born Again Christians with all that entails politically and socially. They live in a small and sheltered world. My examination of their fear-based existence tells me that something is being repressed with these folks. The Big Picture of our family and the way it manifests in their lives indicates to me that something major happened to all of us, not just me. I just acted out in a different manner.

My mother was big on keeping up the charade of respectability while behaving otherwise. I am positive today that she had multiple flirtations, if not actual affairs. I was an empathic child and saw/felt this disconnect. When I would innocently ask her about something I saw she would tell me I was wrong; that I did not see what I so clearly saw but didn't understand. It made me feel crazy inside. Like something was wrong with me. Today she is old and suffering from dementia and occasionally lets a truth slip out. I now know that I did see what I saw and knew what I knew and am finally validated.

My final comment has to do with the label "masochistic." I may have acted out in a similar manner to those who have been molested, but I really don't think my behavior was much unlike many of my peers. Given the broad view of my generation, and knowing the past youthful

25

behavior of my current friends, I would say that my behavior with "bad boys" and such was pretty typical for that late '60s, early '70s era. I needed to push it as far as I could push it. It was the dawning of sex, drugs and rock and roll. Women's lib was developing new opinions about what was acceptable. It may not have been acceptable to older folks, but my behavior, though it may have been masochistic and indicative of psychological problems, was not out of line with the behavior of my peers.

Looking backward, I can see that the period when that dream was prominent in my therapy sessions with you, was a time of change and awakening. I was dropping the veil and accessing my unconscious knowledge, waking up to the truth about much of my psychological situation. Given that emerging growth, I think the 'slave girl' dream might be seen in another way. I offer to you my conclusions about what that dream may have meant at that time.

In the dream, things seem good at first. There is luxury and adventure. I am comfortable, fed, taken care of, albeit in some sort of prison. Just like my stable middle-class family life. Just like my marriage. But then, I start to become more aware. Not to be too Freudian about it, but underground caverns certainly sound like the depths of the unconscious. It is in this cave that I become aware of the danger of staying in this situation. That is, as I continue with my therapy, I see that my family of origin may not be safe after all. I first idolize my parents, then come to learn family secrets, notice cover-ups, see that behavior does not match my friends' families, etc. I don't know things for sure, but I begin to feel that things aren't right. I start to get wise though work in analysis and see the situation for the danger that it potentially poses. One could say this summarizes my marriage as well. I had originally entered therapy because my marriage was falling apart. I felt guilty and "bad" that I wanted to leave such a "perfect guy," but again, as time went on through therapy, I gained a confidence that maybe I wasn't such a bad person and maybe this marriage really was the trap it felt like, a velvet prison of my husband's design.

Thus, in the dream, the young girl starts to sense that something is not right with this situation and has to figure out how to get out of there before she dies. Before she is sacrificed to the gods of convention and propriety. It certainly played out that I did wake up to the danger of the status quo, did escape and save my life by sticking with our therapy and working on myself.

Comparing Emily's new account with my earlier version I am convinced that she has arrived at a more complete version of the truth.

In my 1980 article, I did not use the term "molestation" but spoke of a "sexualized" closeness with her grandfather. That may have been because, just finishing my training at a Freudian institute, I felt I had to give more emphasis to sexuality. In my more recent version, speculating about a "molestation" may have come from all the attention in recent years to child molestations that were covered up. I also agree with her that the term "masochism" is misplaced since it carries too much old Freudian baggage. I think her final version, which lays out the dynamics of the whole family—including her mother's gas-lighting of her—rings true; it gives the fullest understanding of her behavior during the time she saw me in analysis. There may even have been some of my own tacit acceptance of the idea that a woman should stay home while her husband worked that interfered with my questioning how "perfect" her marriage was. Just before the manuscript went to press I received an additional message from Emily in which she reported that her mother, now senile and talking freely, said that her grandfather—who Emily did not know—"touched me and hurt me when I was a child," and that she suffered repeated sexual abuse herself when she was young, thus giving a final confirmation to Emily's belief that her mother was hiding something like this from her when she was growing up. This whole interchange shows the value of back and forth work in which we eventually arrived at a more complete and valid account.

"Bernie" was a businessman I saw for a little over two years, once a week, ending in 1993. This report differs from all the others presented here since I had some trouble tracking him down, wrote my account of what I remembered of his therapy before hearing from him, and then received his version later. We subsequently had an e-mail dialogue; what follows is the result of combining these accounts. Bernie came for treatment because fairly intense anxiety prevented him from falling asleep at night and, the more he struggled with it, the more anxious he became. These panic attacks coincided with his breaking his leg while playing ball with his buddies; he had to wear a cast for some weeks, although he had been informed that his leg would heal without complications, as it eventually did. At first, it was a mystery to him why his injury, if indeed that was the cause, should have unleashed so much fear.

Bernie was the very model of a nice guy, which had served him well in the large corporation where he worked, although he was somewhat naive psychologically. He attempted to figure out the source of his anxiety, talking to one friend at work who had some experience with therapy, and then came to see me. While medication eventually enabled him to sleep and alleviated the anxiety, he continued in therapy, dealing with other difficulties in his life. In my initial version of his panic attacks, I placed major weight on the way his extremely intrusive and controlling mother had shaped his life, how being somewhat immobilized by the cast on his leg aroused fear that she could interfere with his autonomy. He did not completely agree with this, but did feel that his childhood relationship with his mother left him feeling vulnerable and that the feeling of extreme vulnerability, set off by his injury and partial immobilization, was the source of the anxiety. In addition, we explored issues that arose in his job, and what was missing in his marriage to a very passive, emotionally unresponsive woman.

Understanding his panic in terms of feelings of vulnerability seemed to help, though I could never be sure how much. More important for the alleviation of his symptoms were anti-anxiety medication and just having someone to talk with, which he had not had much opportunity to do in his life.

When I wrote my initial report, I did not feel there was a very strong personal connection with Bernie; it seemed I could have been anyone, one of the guys he knew at work, a fellow ball-player, or some other doctor. Typically, he called me "doctor" and not Lou, as most of my other patients did. More searching self-exploration and forming a closer relationship were things that did not occur as much as they did with other patients, or so I thought. In the light of his own later comments, it appears that we simply had different takes on the patient–therapist relationship, mine being that it could develop in a more open, friendly direction and his, that doctor and patient were supposed to remain somewhat formal as intimate personal matters were discussed. He would have welcomed a more personal connection if he thought that was possible. While, in my initial account, I thought his therapeutic gains were modest, his own report reveals that he got a great deal more out of our work than I remembered. Here is his version, written seventeen years after we finished:

> I am struggling with what to write. When I think back about that time of my life and my experience with therapy, the following thoughts come to mind. There felt like there were two components to the experience. The first dealt with what I would call more short-term life issues. I was struggling with issues regarding my marriage, my job and my son. I recall having the feeling of a "safe harbor." The sessions were a

place to go and a person to talk to where I could peel back my layers and speak freely about these issues to a non-judgmental listener. Other than my friend at work there was no other place to do this. From that perspective, it was a good outlet for me. It was not so much as coming up with solutions for those issues as it was just to be able to articulate them to another person. I guess you could think of it in terms of a place to vent. Perhaps a more "psychological" description would be a place to let out thoughts and feelings that otherwise would remain bottled inside me.

The second component was a deeper examination of who I am and why I might react to things in certain ways. More of the "analysis" aspect of the sessions. Although, I do not remember any huge "breakthroughs," I do believe that: (1) I got a better understanding of the long range effects on my personality that resulted from having a mother who always believed she was right. (2) A perspective on growing up being a middle child, which I had not thought about before. (3) How and why I developed a reoccurring need to try to please others.

As for the process itself, I recall having the desire for as much interactivity as possible. I did not want a passive session where I did all the talking. I was looking for input and responses. I believe I expressed this and the Dr. attempted to accommodate my request. Is this helpful at all?

It is interesting that Bernie singles out catharsis, having a safe person to talk with, and insights—in that order—as the helpful factors in his therapy. He eventually got a divorce, seems happy with his life now, is not interested in remarrying, and has become very close with his adult children. Clearly, Bernie got a great deal more out of the therapy than I was aware of. His account—which does not even refer to the panic attacks—shows an important growth in his understanding of himself, his childhood, and the experiences that shaped his personality. This shows the value of a collaborative approach in formulating a case history, of evaluating therapy with the patient's recollections as well as the therapist's, which can produce surprises and a deeper knowledge of the other person.

4

Psychoanalysis Old and New

My memory is that he said virtually nothing the entire time I saw him. He was a very kind person, but as far as having a conversation with him, it was a pretty one-way street. I talked and he [her previous psychoanalyst] listened and nodded...Certainly I spent a lot of time talking about my mother and family, but I can't recall anything he ever said in response.

—Lark

It was communicated to me that I should see myself as a selfish, greedy, raging, envious, malicious, jealous, weak little boy who only wanted what he wanted because he was motivated to kill to satisfy his inbuilt instinctual urges...I do not know how anyone can actually get better and grow as a person from this kind of treatment.

—Nino

Successful therapeutic outcomes depend more on the kind of person the therapist/analyst is than his or her theory-based technique. All the same, good theories can be very useful while bad theories make it difficult, though not impossible, for even the most skillful therapists to be of help. To come at it a different way, much depends on the *match*—or mismatch—between therapist and patient. Judith, described in Chapter 2, got a great deal out of what was a more or less old-style psychoanalysis, while Scott, seen about the same time, wasn't making much progress until I changed my approach. A good illustration of the importance of the match comes from Freud's own psychoanalytic treatment of four patients seen when he was at the height of his powers.[1] With two of these—a young man named Albert Hirst and the psychiatrist Abram Kardiner—there was a good match and the analyses were very successful, while, with two others—James Strachey and John Rickman—their treatments were either bland and meaningless or unhelpful. These different outcomes—all based on the same theory—depended on whether Freud identified with and liked the patient or not: whether there was a good match or mismatch between them, whether he was flexible, or adhered to his technical rules.

Albert Hirst came to see Freud at age twenty-three suffering from a number of serious symptoms, including sexual inhibitions and a suicide attempt. His mother was strict, cold, and opposed to pleasure; he felt she did not love him, while his father was distant and punitive. Freud clearly took a liking to the young man—perhaps he identified with his sexual difficulties—while being venerated certainly appealed to him. What was helpful, which we know from Hirst's own recollections some years later, were things Freud did that in no way followed his own psychoanalytic rules.

Hirst was fifteen minutes late for each of his early sessions but Freud did not interpret this as resistance. He often praised and encouraged the young man, reassured him that his feelings were real and sincere, told him he had talent in interpreting his own dreams, and valued his discussions of novels. Freud had seen Hirst's domineering older sister briefly and told Hirst that he was more intelligent than she and spoke of his unusually good mind, adding, "You aren't a weak person, you are very strong." All these supportive comments had a great impact on Hirst since he believed they were the words of a genius. What was helpful in this good match was the young man's relationship with a man he idolized: someone who took a keen interest in him, praised his abilities, gave reassurance and advice about his sexual difficulties, in short, filled the role of a caring and guiding parent, providing what was lacking in Hirst's own family. Freud was never "abstinent," "neutral," nor a "blank screen," nor was he "anonymous." He talked openly about his own feelings, prejudices, and experiences, and it was all these decidedly nonpsychoanalytic interchanges that Hirst recalled as most helpful.

The next patient to have a positive experience with Freud was the American psychiatrist Abram Kardiner, seen in 1921. Kardiner grew up as a poor Jewish boy in the slums of New York City under extremely traumatic conditions, barely surviving his mother's early death from tuberculosis and his father's violence. As he put it, "My early childhood was a ceaseless nightmare, with starvation, neglect, a sense of being of no account, and a bewildering depressive feeling." Having listened to this account during the first session, Freud told him that it was "a perfect presentation." It seems clear that Freud—whose own Jewish childhood was marred by poverty and his mother's unavailability due, in part, to tuberculosis—felt a real emotional connection with Kardiner.

This identification is what made for the good match between patient and analyst, leading Freud to be openly supportive and encouraging, telling his patient at one point that "he had a lot of fight in him and he would be down at times but he would never be out."

The experience of James Strachey and John Rickman—who became the translators of Freud's works into English (the well-known *Standard Edition*)—seen at the same time, were far different. These two analysands were amazed when Kardiner told them that Freud talked to him since, in their analyses, he was almost always silent. In fact, Rickman reported that the Professor often fell asleep during his sessions. It is doubtful if they got very much from these treatments, but they took Freud's way of working with them as a model and imported the idea of the largely silent analyst back to London. My own sense is that Freud felt no connection with these Oxford- and Cambridge-educated, upper-class Englishmen, with backgrounds so distant from his own: they were just not a good match.

The four cases to be discussed now involve patients, two of whom—"Andrew" and "Lark"—saw classical Freudian analysts, and two—"Nino" and "Elizabeth"—who saw Kleinians, before coming to see me. Their analyses—although not typical of every classical or Kleinian treatment—reveal the worst of these traditional approaches.

Let me begin with the case of Andrew—a highly intelligent, sensitive man, as well as an experienced psychotherapist—who was quite depressed, in fact contemplating suicide, when he came to see me. I saw him for three years, four times a week, lying on the couch, ending in August of 1992. In response to my questionnaire, he first recounted his experience with the two psychoanalysts he had seen just before we began:

> *In my early forties, my life was at a very low ebb. I had spent nine fruitless months in psychoanalytic psychotherapy with a highly regarded psychiatrist and then another fruitless year with an equally regarded psychoanalytic psychologist. [These analyses]...were characterized by a respectful and distant demeanor on the part of the therapists. Throughout the first experience, I felt increasingly depressed and hopeless about my depression. Finally, after about nine months, I told the analyst that I felt he didn't know how to help me and that I wanted to terminate treatment. His response was consistent with his behavior throughout the preceding nine months. First, he paused while he reflected. Then he said, "You feel I cannot help you."*

"Yes, that's right."

After another pause, "I want to be able to help you."

"I believe you do want to help me, but I feel worse than I did and I think you don't know how to help me."

After another pause, "I would like to be able to help you."

This conversation meant to me that, as usual, he was respectful of my experience and, also, as usual, he did not know what to do about it. The conversation did not inspire confidence in me. Rather, it confirmed my pessimism and I terminated treatment.

Soon, I began treatment with another analyst who was also highly regarded in the therapeutic community. Though I initially felt some connection with her, I soon felt, as I had with the previous therapist, that she really did not know what to do to help me feel less depressed. She had the habit—unusual in my experience—of transcribing our conversations on a shorthand tablet. Without fail, when I spoke, she would take down what I said. Or, at least, I assumed that was what she was writing. Perhaps I was mistaken; maybe she was working on a book. Initially, I felt flattered that my words were worth noting. Soon, though, I felt that the ever-present notebook was a barrier between us. She never inquired on its effect on me and I never ventured to tell her.

After nearly a year, feeling more deeply depressed and still feeling that she did not know how to help me feel better, I told her I wanted to terminate treatment. Though her demeanor was usually very similar to that of the previous analyst, her response in this instance was different. She was clearly angry with me. I don't remember much of what she had said in the months of therapy, but I distinctly recall what she said to me that day. "If I'd known you were only interested in the short-term treatment of your depression, I'd have never agreed to see you."

Given that these two analysts practiced according to classical rules, it is safe to assume that they were relatively silent, searched for the childhood origins of Andrew's depression, and focused their interpretations on the transference: the relationship between patient and analyst. Andrew's depression had been set off when his wife, whom he deeply loved, left him for another partner—an unexpected and devastating blow—and while his previous analysts no doubt allowed him to talk about this, it would not have been at the forefront of their understanding of his difficulties. The final response of his second analyst confirms this point. Andrew's experiences with these two psychoanalysts illustrate how a patient is plugged into a fixed slot, his individuality ignored. There was essentially no relationship with him as a unique person; he felt that he, as an individual, was not responded to, while he had a very different experience in our work.

> *In our first visit, I described my prior two very disappointing thera-*
> *peutic experiences and the corresponding pessimism I felt about*
> *therapy for me. I was gratified and, I think, a little surprised, when*
> *you confirmed my views of the two previous therapists.* [I knew of
> these psychoanalysts from colleagues in the community.] *Finding my*
> *experience thus validated was the first meaningful experience I had*
> *in what would prove to be a very effective treatment.*
>
> *My predominant sense of my psychoanalysis is of developing more*
> *self-acceptance. There is nothing particular I remember about the*
> *treatment that led to that. Two memories stand out, however. A few*
> *months into treatment, I described having had too much to drink*
> *the night before. As Lou saw me to the door at the end of the hour,*
> *he said, gently, "And don't drink too much tonight." This was such a*
> *simple, human thing to say and, perhaps, because it was simple and*
> *human—and not strategic nor otherwise "clinically sophisticated"—I*
> *felt his concern but not his criticism. A couple of years into treatment,*
> *Lou handed me a plate of chocolate chip cookies, saying something*
> *like, "My wife baked these for you."* [This was in response to his talking,
> in an earlier session, about one of his rare happy childhood memories
> in which he was given some cookies.] *I was touched by their shared*
> *generosity. This isn't a typical clinical intervention, but it had the*
> *effect, nonetheless, of conveying human interest in me.*
>
> *As I write this, I am struck by repetition of the word "human." I have*
> *had many experiences of various kinds of psychotherapy over the*
> *years, and this experience is one in which the humanity of the thera-*
> *pist was particularly vivid. I realize that my memories of this therapy*
> *don't refer to clinical methodology or skill. This may be, in part, be-*
> *cause the methodology, as I recall it, was so deeply embedded in the*
> *humanness of the interaction. I have often pondered the question of*
> *what was effective about the particular way that Lou related to me,*
> *because, on the one hand, it was not unusual or special—compared*
> *with that of some psychotherapists I have known. What is clear to me*
> *is that Lou's approach reflected an unusual grasp of the sometimes*
> *evanescent distinction between being too distant and too intimate.*
> *Achieving this appropriate distance is, surely, a struggle engaged*
> *in by all serious, caring, responsible therapists, but it is a struggle,*
> *nonetheless. So, in my view, as a patient and as a clinician, achieving*
> *this rightness of distance reflects a particular grace.*

As Andrew's depression lifted, he began dating and eventually fell in love with a wonderful and caring woman to whom he remains happily married. He and his new wife moved to a distant city. His creativity—writing, photography—has flowered, and his depression has not returned in the eighteen years since the end of his therapy.

"Lark" was a woman in her early thirties when she came to see me, after moving to Los Angeles from another city where she had been in analysis with a young man who was in training at the Freudian Institute there. The fact that he was in training and supervision no doubt led him to be even more silent and "classical" then he may have become later. Despite her intelligence, gentle manner, attractiveness, professional training, and job in a high-powered firm, she felt inadequate and unlovable, which led her into a disastrous marriage with the first man who showed an interest in her. "Howard," initially her boyfriend and then her husband, was also in a classical analysis in that city and continued with another senior Freudian after they moved to Los Angeles. Lark had suffered from depression since adolescence, which seemed the result of growing up with a cold, critical, and rejecting mother and "nice" but ineffectual father. Her brother was the family prince, while she was relegated to neglect in her basement bedroom. Here is her account of her previous analysis as well as her work with me:

> I've been thinking about this the last few days and my memories of the guy I saw in "A" for five years are pretty sharp even though so much time has passed, because my experience of him was so consistent from week to week. Although, of course, it can't be true, my memory is that he said virtually nothing the entire time I saw him. I have never met a quieter person in my life. I used to imagine that he was lively and engaged in his home life, but those fantasies were never very long lasting, because it was so preposterous. I know that's silly, but it was my fantasy... He was a very kind person, but as far as having a conversation with him, it was a pretty one-way street. I talked and he listened and nodded.
>
> I remember that one week he handed me the check I had mailed to him, because I had forgotten to sign it. That gesture seemed to have some meaning, but again, I felt it was up to me to interpret it. I guess I probably was angry at him for not talking to me, but I think the check was just a mistake... I had to deal with so much conflict at work, that if the point of my therapy with him was to get angry, that was a failure from the first session. Certainly I spent a lot of time talking about my mother and family, but I can't recall anything he ever said in response.

My years in A were not happy, no surprise, as I worked in a very stressful, super competitive firm with several bullies. I was either complaining about my job, my unhappy relationship with Howard, or complaining about how lonely I was after we broke up. I went through an abortion when Howard and I were together and I really cannot recall one word my analyst said that was either supportive or judgmental. I know I felt very dependent on him because I had done such a poor job of making a life for myself outside of work and work always felt like a combat zone. The only time I can remember that he ever challenged my thinking about anything was when, after months of hearing me whine about my loneliness, I told him about some guy coming up to me at a concert and trying to initiate a conversation. I related how timid I felt and he basically said "well how are you going to meet anyone if you don't talk to people?" A sensible question indeed. Looking back at that time in my life I can't believe how stuck I was—and only thirty! I can now think of fifty things I could have done to get out of that rut. Although I was depressed, I wish he could have challenged my self-pity more. Maybe that is hard to do while being supportive of a depressive...I don't know.

Howard saw some guy in the Freudian institute for several years: on the couch and everything. I think it's safe to say it did not give him much insight. When he moved to L.A. he saw another Freudian, because I recall that he was a big shot in the L.A. institute...and had virtually the same experience. I remember hearing Howard talk about who was the "best" analyst and know there was a lot of elitism amongst those guys.

Anyway, I know this is not why you are asking for this recollection, but it does remind me of my gratitude to you for your work with me. I felt like you struck a very good balance between giving advice and letting me draw my own conclusions. I appreciated your unequivocal advice to stay away from my mother, yet didn't ever feel like I couldn't, for example, tell you about being sucked back into her web. Lou, I also really appreciated your honesty with me about Howard. I remember when we were seeing you together, one of us, probably me, asked you, essentially, if there was any hope for our relationship. You said "yes." I believe that was because you saw the traits and shared experiences that drew us together originally and that was the basis of your answer. Of course, I am even more grateful for your support through all the crap with Howard. I always felt supported by you and that you "heard" me. I also appreciated being able to talk about books with you, especially when I was sick of talking about my family, [we still mail each other books now and then.] *I appreciated your sense of humor and also that you were sufficiently tolerant of my besotted state as a new mother to let me bring my newborn daughter in to show you. And my sister and new husband-to-be, too. It made me feel like I could show you all the important parts of my life.*

I saw Lark for thirteen years, once and occasionally twice, a week. She also went on antidepressant medication, which she found helpful. Meanwhile, Howard continued his fruitless work with a classical analyst. She and I came up with a plan: I would see them as a couple—which was a good idea in any case—and this would give Howard the idea that there were other forms of analytic therapy that could be helpful. The plan worked on both counts. Howard, who suffered from severe bulimia that was never even mentioned, much less dealt with, in either of his previous analyses, could see what was missing in those treatments and took my referral to a colleague. And, after some months of couple's therapy, it was clear that they were not compatible and got a divorce. Lark has since moved back to her hometown, is re-married, and, despite some troubles with her children that seem to be working out, has survived a number of difficulties, done well in her career, and, most significantly, is not depressed.

"Nino" was a therapist in his early forties when he first came to see me in 2002. I saw him once a week for a bit less than two years, tapering off to once a month, and stopping in March of 2005. He had been in a Kleinian analysis for five years, more then twenty years earlier, and, just before seeing me, had worked with an older psychiatrist who had converted to self-psychology from his earlier Freudian orientation. Since the influence of Melanie Klein remains widespread—especially in England and South America—it will be worth presenting Nino's experience with that form of analysis, as well as his comparison of his more recent therapy with our work.

I endured a strict Kleinian psychoanalysis for nearly six years. Having little knowledge of this theoretical persuasion, I had no idea of what I would be subjected to. I had come into treatment with issues related to being overprotected by a very anxious mother, and a generally uninvolved father. This had created various problems with passivity, compliance, and doing things that others wanted me to do instead of what I wanted. I had suffered from depression since late adolescence. I was hoping that, from this treatment, I would be able to develop some strength of character, what I would today call an empowered sense of self.

I soon found out that my analyst had his own agenda. He was very aloof, actually kind of interpersonally weird. His emotions were very stilted. He rarely smiled and usually had a kind of poker face when he would greet me at the door. He would walk in front of me to his seat behind the couch, and I would dutifully follow. He never turned around to look at me. When the session was over, he would remain seated until I left the office.

During sessions he would remain quiet until I had talked for quite awhile, then he would interpret most everything I said. He didn't relate the content to anything that was going on with me in the circumstances that I was describing, but about my relationship with him. He took the usual accusatorial line that I was in some way, envious of him, greedy of what he had, hateful of his superior position in my life, destructive, angry and all in all just negative to him. He saw my frustration with him as related to these internal feelings that were really directed at my parents. I saw them as being related to his dreadful descriptions of me. I experienced strongly that he did not know "me"; that he could not have an understanding of what was important to me. I do not remember anything impactful coming out of talking about the actual events with my parents that had pressured me into the behavioral outcomes in my life. The treatment really got bizarre when he felt that I was ready to be confronted with the "body-parts" accusations. I was told that I wanted his "breasts," his penis, and most of all, his "penis in his breast."[2] He did not explain the dubious meanings of all this. At the time, I did not get what he was trying to get me to understand at all. It was really quite comical, but since I was still quite depressed, I tried not to think that this was a waste of time. I kept hoping that something magical would happen from what he was telling me; that something would click from my "unconscious" and I would feel better. For the last two years of my analysis—five days a week—90% of the time was spent on dream analysis. I finally realized that I was not going to get better in this very foreign and strange treatment. After a particularly insulting interpretation about an inflamed prostate I was suffering from, I got up from the couch at the end of the session, turned around, and told him "good-bye"; my usual comment had been "I'll see you tomorrow." I did not return the next day and have not talked to him for nearly twenty years.

I did not experience a human relationship in this treatment. There was very little empathy, very little attunement to what I was saying and the affects that they were bringing up in me. In the third month of treatment he told me to stop crying so much. It seemed "forced" to him. He did not want to find out why my tears came so easy and were so strong; I was suffering from a major depressive episode and it hurt. I very rarely cried again in the more than five years that I stayed in treatment. I complied with what he said about me and did not tell him how weird I thought the things he was telling me about myself were, or, actually, how weird I thought he was. When one time I met him in the elevator coming back from the cafeteria in the office building he seemed uncomfortable having a normal conversation with me. He was holding a hamburger, I literally thought to myself "My God, he eats; he must be a real person!" This would have been good "grist for the mill" in our session that day, but I dared not bring it up; there was too much of a possibility that he would accuse me of something that was part of my murderous rage toward him.

I do not feel he ever got close to any of my salient issues from my development. I did learn to be more assertive, after my depression spontaneously lifted five years into the analysis, which allowed me to leave him. The only rage I was conscious of was the fact that I spent over $90,000 for all of this.

It was communicated to me that I needed to have a different perspective about myself; that I should see myself as a selfish, greedy, raging, envious, malicious, jealous, weak little boy who only wanted what he wanted because he was motivated to kill to satisfy his inbuilt instinctual urges. In fact, I never recalled any fantasies about destroying my mother or father. I do not know how anyone can actually get better and grow as a person from this kind of treatment.

Lest the reader find this Kleinian treatment outlandish, Nino's description is consistent with others I have heard. Many years after quitting this first treatment, Nino made a second attempt at therapy, this time with a self-psychologist. Here is his account of that experience as well as his description of his work with me:

He began by describing a formative adolescent experience in which he felt forced to break off a relationship with the first girl he loved because, as a dutiful Catholic boy, he could see that they were about to engage in forbidden sex. He retained a vivid memory of her telling him he had "beautiful eyes."

I knew that God would not be very happy with me if I had indulged my desires before I was married. The biggest reason, though, was that I would not have been able to tolerate the tremendous guilt my mother would have rained upon me if she found out that I had become sexually active as a teenager and, of course, that I was not

*married. The loss of my first love, by my own doing, affected how
I viewed myself and my subsequent relationships with women until
I entered psychoanalytic psychotherapy with Dr. Breger.*

*I had been in two separate psychoanalyses which totaled nearly ten
years without their touching on the importance of the above incident
for my life.[3] My second analysis was with a psychiatrist who identified
himself as a self-psychologist. Though he listened to the story of my
first love, and interpreted dreams about her, he never applied them
to me in a way that I saw the tremendous importance she still had for
me in my life. During this treatment I was having some difficulties in
my marriage that revolved around sex and, in hindsight; I can see how
the template of so many years ago was affecting me in the present. I do
not know why there was not more importance placed on this during
this second treatment. My feeling is that it was up to me to find out
the connections by myself instead of there being a collaborative effort
made by my analyst and me.*

*The result of not becoming aware of the magnitude of leaving my first
love in the way that I did was that I became involved in a protracted
affair that has brought near tragic results in my life. It was after I
had been involved in this affair that, upon entering treatment with
Dr. Breger, I grew to understand the connection between the two
women* [his adolescent girlfriend and the woman he had the affair
with] *who both thought that I had "beautiful eyes." The secret of the
treatment was that this time I was followed very closely about what
my first love meant to me, what I had experienced with her, and how
this loss was not mourned. That the regrets over having given up my
teenage love were never understood, so that they remained in an
idealized, guilt-ridden state that kept me from wanting to fulfill these
legitimate longings in my marriage. Dr. Breger's interpretations simply
followed the material. They deeply resonated with me. He did not put
anything on me or "into" me. He listened and remembered aspects of
my life that made sense with understanding why I had made decisions in my life that brought so much pain. His willingness to let the
treatment be worked out together, that I could run with his insights,
altering them when they did not feel right, helped in finding my way
to a better understanding of the particular needs and vulnerabilities
I have. I only wish that I had worked on all this sooner.*

Elizabeth was a young, married, graduate student in clinical
psychology who I saw for three years, once a week, ending in October
of 1992. She initially sought therapy as a requirement of her training
program. She was quite accomplished, a fine pianist, had done her

undergraduate work at an Ivy League school, and was doing very well in her graduate program. Her marriage seemed relatively untroubled. In other words, she was functioning at a very high level and, if there was anything that she needed psychotherapy for, it was to modify her need to be perfect. The one theme that stands out in my memory was the fact that she had a brother, born with a very serious congenital illness, who took up a great deal of her parents' time and attention. Her father was also showing the early signs of dementia, which was of real concern to her. She became pregnant during the last year of our work together and, at one of our final sessions, brought her new infant son in for me to see. Upon completion of her Ph.D., she and her husband decided to move to a smaller eastern city since it seemed a better place to raise children. I subsequently heard, via a Christmas card, that she had put her career aside to stay home and care for her two children in their early years. This was a decision she made on her own, after the completion of therapy, although her seeking emotional fulfillment in motherhood does relate to things we worked on. Here is her own account, written more than eighteen years after the completion of our work:

> While you're not asking about my work with other psychologists, it's impossible to think of our work together outside the context of my previous therapy experiences. I entered psychotherapy while I was a student in a clinical psychology Ph.D. program. Some months of therapy was a program requirement, and I was also motivated by a desire to grow in self-awareness. I had never been in prior psychotherapy—although in looking back, there are times when I think it would have benefited me.
>
> The first psychologist I saw was someone recommended by a classmate. During my initial session with her, I said that I was working with young children who had been sexually abused. The therapist asked if I found this work difficult because of my own childhood history of abuse. I was a little taken aback, but stated that my history did not include abuse. The interview proceeded, and she made another reference or two to the challenges of doing clinical work with patients whose issues mirrored my own, particularly when those issues involved sexual abuse. I remember thinking at the time that she was a bit of a nut. I did not schedule another appointment with her.
>
> Next I sought a referral from one of my professors, an engaging and challenging teacher with Kleinian inclinations. I scheduled an appointment with the therapist she recommended. In my first session,

this second psychologist prompted, "Did you have a dream?" I did. She listened attentively, and then offered some interpretations. When I told her that the interpretations didn't really resonate, she explained that this was due to my resistance. This irritated me. She explained that my irritation was an indication that her interpretation had touched a nerve, and that we were, therefore, on the right track. Knowing that my professor would only recommend someone really good, I thought perhaps the psychotherapist was right. I continued seeing her for several months. The sessions were always the same—I would begin by talking about events in my life—she would listen impatiently and eventually interrupt me with, "Did you have a dream?" I would tell a dream, and she would offer interpretations about my rage. I wasn't aware of the rage she referred to, although as our treatment continued I found myself becoming enraged, which seemed to indicate that the treatment was working and that we were really getting at something. I had heard that therapy can be a difficult and painful process, and I was certainly finding this process to be difficult. And maddening. I was also confused, since her interpretations really didn't feel consonant with how I experienced my dreams. Several months into treatment, she confronted me about the treatment fee we had negotiated, explaining that my request to pay her less than her full fee—which seemed reasonable to me, since I was a graduate student—was emblematic of my hostility to her, and my contempt for psychoanalysis. While I had been willing to entertain the notion all along that she knew me better than I knew myself, and that her interpretations only felt wrong because they were really right, this confrontation was the last straw, and I ended the relationship.

By now, I had completed my psychotherapy requirement, but had never felt so angry, so confused about my identity, so distrusting of my own instincts. Whereas before, I had wanted to enter psychotherapy, now I felt like I really needed it. This is the context in which I began my work with you. I still have a distinct impression of your greeting me in your waiting room, extending your hand and saying, "Lou Breger." So simple, but this immediately gave me the feeling that you were a warm and approachable person, a very different vibe from either of the first two therapists.

In my first session—and for many sessions?—I told you about my work with my previous therapist, how angry and confused I was. I half-expected for our starting point in therapy to be your helping me recognize that my previous therapist's assessment of my hostility was, in fact, on track. Instead, you listened to me and affirmed what I was feeling. The way I remember it, you even affirmed that I was right in my assessment of the previous therapist's destructiveness. I felt like you engaged with me in genuine conversation and took me seriously. Throughout the therapy experience with you, I always felt like a person in a relationship, rather than a specimen to be understood by you, and then explained back to me. You listened patiently and non-judgmentally. You treated my own assessments of and insights about my experiences with respect. My sense of your therapeutic stance was that you were looking to me to tell you about myself, and that we would work together to figure things out. I remember talking with you about some turbulence and experiences that occurred during my late adolescence/early adulthood: experiences that were still embarrassing and confusing to me. I looked to you for some sort of judgment, perhaps, or explanation. You said something like, "I think this is a period of your life that we still don't understand very well." This seemingly simple statement stands out to me as the most profound moment in our work together: you communicated an utter lack of judgment, an acceptance of the aspects of my life about which I was the most embarrassed, and modeled that **Not Knowing** *was okay. As a result of that moment—and all the moments in therapy that led up to it—I think I am a more forgiving—and self-forgiving— and accepting—and self-accepting—person.*

My relationship with you was different from other relationships—not only from that with the earlier therapists, but in general. While there is—still!—no sexual or other abuse in my background, I did grow up with a sense of needing to be many things for many people: the loving daughter, top student, outstanding performer, perfect girlfriend. In my therapy with you, you didn't need me to be anything for you. I felt accepted and that you genuinely cared about me. That experience allowed me to be a more authentic person, and I think the way I live my life and my current relationships reflect that. It's a process and still a work in progress.

Thanks for giving me the opportunity to gather some of my thoughts and memories, and to put them into writing.—Elizabeth

Elizabeth still has a loving relationship with her husband, the baby she brought to a session is now a freshman at her alma mater, and both her son and daughter continue the family's interest in music, as does Elizabeth. She has chosen not to practice psychotherapy but has become a college teacher of psychology, which she finds very fulfilling, along with involvement in professional organizations. Her first therapist was probably trying to force her to acknowledge sexual abuse that never happened, which was all the rage among some therapists for a brief period, while her second was laying on the same Kleinian interpretations that we saw in the case of Nino. I think Elizabeth's comments on the acceptance of herself and others shows that she has moved beyond the demands for perfection that were so prominent when she began her therapy with me. Interestingly, the effects of her brother's illness, which I remembered as prominent in our work, were not mentioned by her.

These cases illustrate the kind of contemporary analytic therapy I practice, even though the early ones were seen before I could fully articulate my ideas. Andrew and Lark's descriptions of their unsatisfactory experiences with their largely silent and theory-bound psychoanalysts are quite similar and illustrate the worst of classical Freudian practice. Nino's description of his Kleinian analysis is on another planet, though I sometimes think of this as the Freudian theory-driven approach taken to an absurd extreme. Elizabeth's brief experience with a Kleinian therapist was much the same at Nino's. It is important to note that, while both the Freudian and Kleinian approaches advocate "free association," in all four of these cases the patients did not feel free to talk about how their analysts affected them in the sessions. Andrew—who had a good deal of prior experience as both a patient and therapist himself—did break off the two treatments after some months, though he never told his second analyst how he felt about her intrusive notebook. Elizabeth also stopped her treatment fairly quickly when her first two therapists tried to force ideas on her that did not fit her experience. But Lark and Nino stayed with their silent Freudian and weird Kleinian analysts for more than five years, hoping that something would happen, that their depressions would lift, and they never told them how they felt about the silence or the insulting interpretations. They were compliant: not free to express what they felt were the most important aspects of their treatments.[4]

My work with all of these patients has much in common. One additional difference between the old and new forms of analysis is worth mentioning, however. While Freud's insight into the formative importance of childhood relationships is one of his most important contributions, it can be overemphasized to the neglect of experiences that occur in later life.[5] Andrew was overcome with depression caused by his wife's desertion, Lark had a terrible time with her job and marriage, and Nino's experience of lost love, at age eighteen, had a long-lasting effect on him. While all these experiences were influenced by what had happened in childhood—Nino's propensity to feel guilty had been instilled in him by his mother since he was a small boy—when they sought treatment, it was the adult difficulties and losses that were most salient. What I did was pay attention as they talked about these experiences and not try to reduce everything they spoke about to childhood antecedents.

To summarize the key elements involved in effective analytic psychotherapy, as illustrated by the nine cases discussed so far, one must remember that every patient is a unique individual. In the cases of Andrew and Elizabeth, I should make clear that I don't talk with everyone about their previous therapists, nor do I give every patient cookies; in fact I can't remember ever having done so with anyone else. Those acts arose from my sense that they were what Andrew and Elizabeth needed. Similarly with Scott, where the work progressed once we were sitting face-to-face and he experienced me as a "friend and supporter," as well as with Bernie, who desired an active give and take. Lark, Nino, and Elizabeth, had previous therapies—with a completely silent Freudians, and theory-bound Kleinians, or a woman who assumed there was sexual abuse when it didn't exist—that were so unhelpful, if not harmful, that my straightforward approach of attending to what they said and what was happening in their lives—Andrew's wife's desertion, a stressful job and a disturbed husband, in the case or Lark, and the traumatic loss of love in adolescence that had never been mourned or integrated, in the case of Nino—was relatively easy to do. It did not mean that I was infallible; I simply listened closely and did not impose rules, techniques, or theoretical dogma. All these therapies were collaborations between two distinct persons, as opposed to a patient with a psychoanalyst who follows a script.

5

Finding My Way

From Ferdinand the Bull to the Lone Ranger

Since contemporary analytic psychotherapy consists of a relationship between two unique individuals, it will be important to understand the kind of person I am. The next three chapters will present some of my own background—both personal and professional—to show how I came to practice my particular version of analytic psychotherapy.

As I look back on my long career as a college professor, psychotherapist, research psychologist, and scholar, it is hard to believe how I got here, starting out as a poor, skinny little boy who struggled, from middle childhood on, with feelings of inferiority. I was born in 1935 in the middle of the Great Depression. Three years before my birth, my parents moved to Los Angeles from New York City with my father's family; my grandparents on both sides were part of the wave of Jewish immigrants who came to America from Europe in the early 1900s. Until my brother was born when I was six, I was the only child of young, physically healthy parents. While we had very little money, and lived in a string of small, shabby apartments, I remember the earliest years as relatively happy times with real closeness and love. This experience left a core of security that accounts for one significant side of my personality.

During my early years, my mother stayed at home with me. Later, despite having a college degree that qualified her as an English teacher, she chose to work part-time in nursery schools. As I came to understand later, she was a deeply impaired person and this was probably all she could manage. My mother was very intelligent, she had skipped two years in elementary school, and was a great reader and lover of books, qualities that I absorbed from her and which were the forerunners of becoming a writer myself. At the same time she had a continuing preoccupation with a plethora of somatic symptoms. I have many childhood memories of going with her to this doctor or that, though no physical illness was ever found. Her many symptoms

47

were the precursors of the major depression that overtook her when I was twenty-five, complete with suicide attempts, hospitalizations, and electric shock treatments. She never really recovered from this depression. Her first breakdown occurred before antidepressant medications were widely available, and she did not make a meaningful connection with the various psychiatrists she saw during her several hospitalizations. Given my early closeness with her, I found her depression, along with my visits to her in mental hospitals, very painful.

Her suicide attempts were all done within the relationship with my father. She would overdose on sleeping pills in the early morning hours so that, when he woke up, he would find her slipping away and have to rush her to the emergency room. She made five such attempts while he was still alive, the last after he retired and was enjoying the one thing he most loved: playing his violin in an amateur chamber music group. This time, when he found her in the afternoon, as he later told me, he vacillated over whether to take her to the hospital or let her die. He finally dropped her off at the emergency room but did not stay with her, being worn down and angry with this hopeless pattern. Later, during this hospitalization, they did get involved in family sessions with a competent social worker, and I sat in on these, hoping that, finally, they could break out of the deadly dance they had been engaged in for so long. But, after a few sessions, my father quit. As he told me shortly thereafter, he had come to feel that it didn't matter if he lived or died. He had had two heart attacks a few years earlier, the second brought on by pushing himself to work too hard in the yard on a hot day and, after her fifth suicide attempt, he brought about his own death by running around at full speed on the tennis court, against his cardiologist's advice. He collapsed on the court with a fatal heart attack.

Like him, as my mother's suicide attempts and hospitalizations were repeated over the years—there were six in all—I became somewhat inured. As I later came to understand her life, I realized that she was a replacement child; the sister born before her had died at age three—the saintly "feigela" or little bird—and she was conceived with the hope of alleviating her mother's sadness, which, as is so often the case, did not work. The new baby did not banish the sadness and, as a replacement, she was both a ghost and a child who must live up to an impossible ideal. My mother grew up with a depressed and unavailable mother and, despite being bright and attractive, had a very lonely, isolated, and unhappy childhood.

While she attempted to have my father play a maternal role with her, he could not really make up for what she missed as a child and she found a particular kind of love with her sensitive little son—me—that was both a blessing and a curse. In the formative earliest years, I felt secure within the family. At the same time, she only loved me as a dependent, unaggressive infant and little boy, and my identity was defined by her in those terms. She would often read me the book *Ferdinand the Bull*, the story of a bull who is so gentle that he refuses to fight, preferring to lie about and smell the flowers. While it is a charming tale, and could be taken as an antiwar manifesto, when given exclusive emphasis, Ferdinand—reinforced by her telling me how I was just like him—was hardly a suitable model for an energetic young male. Her way of defining my identity, which I absorbed in these early years, did not prepare me for the world of boys, aggression, and competition. When I began my schooling, my feelings were easily wounded, tears came quickly, and I feared I would be labeled a crybaby and a sissy.

Around the age of ten or twelve, I made an attempt to change, to give up those things associated with being an overly sensitive little boy. I insisted that everyone call me "Lou" instead of the more childish "Louie," stifled my emotions, and have rarely cried since. In other words, I made a compensation that led to emotional over-control that persists to this day. The Lone Ranger, my favorite radio program in those days before television, became my model, later to be replaced by Gary Cooper in *High Noon*—"yep," "nope"—and Marlon Brando in *Viva Zapata*. All these assertive, heroic men essentially act on their own in their battles against injustice, values that were to appear later in my career as a therapist and writer.

Another way I broke free of my mother's attempt to define me was by bonding with other boys and, later, with men. I always had at least one good male friend, the "guys" to whom this book is dedicated. In chronological order, here are my close male friends, all of whom I am still in touch with. We have listened to and supported each other over the years as we have gone through difficult times: divorces, illnesses, the deaths of parents, struggles with work and creative projects, as well as sharing our plans and aspirations.

Eugene Rosenberg, whom I first met in Junior High in 1948, was my closest friend through Hollywood High, where we played on the basketball team together, worked at summer jobs, towed each other's old cars around Los Angeles when they invariably broke down, and were undergrads at UCLA. Eugene later immigrated to Israel, where he became a world-renowned microbiologist at the University of Tel Aviv. Dan Goldrich was my closest friend in the years at The University of Oregon. We first met in 1962, and he remains there as an emeritus professor of Political Science. He has done important work studying politics aimed at equity, democracy, and sustainability, carried out on a participant observational basis. Sandy Hirshen—"The People's Architect" and my fellow Neatnik—and I met in Berkeley in 1967. Sandy has had a distinguished career as an architect and architectural educator in Berkeley and Vancouver, Canada, designing shelters for migrant workers, facilities for the Navajos in New Mexico, homes for the aged, and low income, socially oriented projects. Robert Rosenstone and I met when I came to Caltech in 1970 and we quickly became close friends with many shared interests. Robert is the author of several fine works of both history and fiction, including *Romantic Revolutionary*—an award winning biography of John Reed—two novels, *King of Odessa* and *Red Star, Crescent Moon—A Muslim Jewish Love Story*, and two books devoted to the historical film. David Markel and I met at the Southern California Psychoanalytic Institute in 1980. Dave and I were central to the founding of The Institute of Contemporary Psychoanalysis (ICP) in 1990, and he, more than anyone else, has worked tirelessly to keep the Institute true to its principles. We remain close friends today.

And the "Sunnyside Boys": "Skin" is Pete Scheiner, my freshman college roommate at Cornell in 1953. He taught me to play the guitar as we listened to Woody Guthrie records, and I spent all the vacation breaks with him in Sunnyside, Queens—a kind of left-wing enclave—where I was accepted into his group of like-minded friends. Pete became a professor of chemistry and is now retired, but still picking away at folk and country music. The Sunnyside group includes Bill Woolf, now retired and a marathon runner; Art Goldberg, also retired, who wrote for *Ramparts* magazine and worked as a community activist; Les Schonbrun, a world class Scrabble player; and Jim Perlstein—"Toad"—a history professor and college union organizer. I reconnected with them in the San Francisco Bay Area in 2004 since, as it happened, Art, Bill and Les all live here and Pete and Jim come out for regular visits. Amazing how we picked up the friendships as if there were no intervening years.

As I moved into the world of school and other children, my perception of my family changed. In the early years, my father seemed like a big, strong man who could do everything. As I grew older—and certainly by adolescence—and began to see him through the eyes of

50

the wider world, I experienced a great disappointment. Because of his self-defeating tendencies, he moved from job to job and, as a boy, I never had an answer to that important question, "What does your Dad do?" It was hard for me to say what he *did* do, but whatever job he briefly held, we never had much money. I have memories of wearing second-hand clothes, playing with cast-off toys, and having to wait forever to get the bicycle I craved. Eventually, he became a social worker, not something men typically did in those years, and certainly not a career that I could identify with at the time. As I grew older, and his own life was more of a disappointment, he was critical and undermining of my efforts to succeed. On the other hand, in his final years, he did seem to find meaningful work as a medical social worker at the City of Hope hospital, working with seriously ill patients and their families. As I look back now, I can see he was a lost soul, struggling with his troubled career, a depressed-suicidal wife, and, in the end, killing himself. After his death, I found some autobiographical notes in which he said that all his life he had been running away from things—his parents, college, his jobs, his wife—but never understood why. Despite my ambivalent feelings toward him, his death was a painful loss and I still find myself thinking of him, more than thirty years later.

Despite the disappointment with my Dad, and his lack of support, I continued to respect and admire some of his qualities: a strong sense of morality and commitment to principles, along with the value of hard work, even though he was never able to channel his efforts into a career that was particularly rewarding. If he was not successful at his job, I would do well at two at the same time: becoming a basketball player *and* guitarist, a writer *and* carpenter, a professor *and* psychotherapist. In short, I became, and remained for many years, a workaholic. While I was somewhat successful as an athlete, guitarist, and carpenter-remodeler, it was only when I became a psychotherapist and scholar that I found my true calling. My father was also a caretaker—with my mother, his social work clients, and his younger siblings—which was another aspect of his character that became part of me on my way to becoming a therapist.

My family's left-wing political beliefs played an important role during my childhood. Like a number of people who suffered the economic hardships of the Great Depression, they were drawn to Communism and, through the 1930s, were members of the Party, though they never did more than go to meetings and read *The Daily People's World*. Being relatively new to Los Angeles, their fellow Party members became their social circle. This was the defining set of ideas that I grew up with; the "working man" was heroic and greedy "capitalists" were bad. Racism was the great evil in America, Paul Robeson was a hero, and, while they didn't care if I used profanity, "nigger" was the worst thing anyone could say. Since religion was "the opiate of the masses," we never so much as entered a synagogue. In other words, while culturally Jewish—I had Yiddish-speaking grandparents named Jake and Becky—the religious side of Judaism was entirely absent from my life. Since we lived in a predominantly Christian, working-class neighborhood, my parent's Communism, along with being Jewish, made me feel like an outsider.

My own reaction to my family's left-wing beliefs was a mixed one. As I got older, many of their friends seemed like oddballs, and I certainly did not want to be like them. At the same time, I admired my father's principles. Both parents were great fans of President Roosevelt and, when the Soviet Union became our ally in the Second World War, "Uncle Joe" Stalin was on our side. What is more, my father really loved America, was devoted to the democratic principles of equality and fair play, and even enlisted in the army at the age of thirty-four in 1945. When he joined the war effort I, aged ten, was very proud of him. During the Cold War in the 1950s, he was called before The House Un-American Activities Committee and refused to give the names of his former Party colleagues—citing the First Amendment as his reason—which led to his losing his job as a social worker with the County Welfare Department, where he was hardly a threat to national security. When I was a freshman in college, following his example, I refused to sign the "loyalty oath" that was required of us in the compulsory Reserve Officer Training Corps (R.O.T.C.) class. So, while I never agreed with Communist ideology—as a college student, I had many arguments with my Dad about various issues in which he blindly followed the Party line—this whole side of life in the family left me with a predisposition to think critically, to challenge established beliefs, to go my own way, identify with "the little guy," the poor, the less powerful, and the dispossessed.

As I moved into adolescence, I took up sports with a vengeance. By the age of fourteen I settled on basketball and spent countless hours perfecting my skills. In my senior year in high school, I made the varsity team and should have been first string given the level of my play during practice. But then my unconscious took over. Despite my ability,

I would always choke up in the actual games and not do as well as I should. I was demoted and spent most of the time on the bench. The meaning of this pattern was revealed to me much later, for example, in this dream from my thirties:

> *I am playing in a basketball game, grab a rebound and dribble rapidly down the court. I am being followed by a woman in a dragon-lady dress who looks like the black congresswoman Shirley Chisholm. I think, "She won't be able to stop me, especially not with that ridiculous dress." I drive to the basket, jump to shoot my lay up, when she rises behind and blocks my shot. How humiliating!*

Shirley Chisholm is tied to my parent's radical politics and her glasses are like those my mother always wore. Clearly, it is my mother who is behind my inability to do well as a basketball player. The same unconscious dynamic was also apparent in my relations with women. Like many adolescent boys, I was preoccupied with girls and sex. Yet, in some way I did not understand, I was too anxious to even talk to most of them and was convinced that no girl I found attractive would like me. So here again, as with basketball, the unconscious legacy of my relationship with my mother lived on and interfered with my achieving my potential. And it really wasn't conscious; I had no idea why I always got so anxious in basketball games or why I was convinced that no girl would respond to me. The unconscious message was that I should remain a gentle little boy—a Ferdinand—to become an assertive man was threatening; if I did, I would lose my mother's love.

Things like this are always more complicated, of course. While I was hampered by these internal blocks, I also fought against them. After high school, I decided to go to a college as far away as I could and was fortunate to be admitted to Cornell University.[1] At Cornell, I made the freshman basketball team and, at first, the old pattern continued, and I was demoted from the starting five. But, finally, in a game against a good team, I broke free and played up to my potential. I performed well for the rest of the season, but this was the high point of my basketball career. I realized that I didn't have the athletic skills to do more than excel on the freshman team at an Ivy League school and, while I loved basketball, it became a hobby; I played in pick-up and playground games until my late thirties. I worked hard at my studies, did reasonably well academically, came home after my freshman year, and transferred to UCLA. There, I eventually overcame my shyness and became emotionally and sexually involved with women.

Academic achievement was the final aspect of the neurosis I carried from my childhood. While I can look back now and realize that I have achieved professional success in two areas, as an undergraduate, I was much more uncertain. Unlike the typical Jewish parents, mine never pushed their first-born son to do well in school: in fact, they didn't seem all that interested. As I realized much later, both of them felt diminished by my success; they were not happy if I did well, either athletically or academically. My mother would never fail to comment on my inability to spell: "So, the great college professor and writer of books, and he still can't spell." (Which I still can't: thank God for spell check). I used to joke that my mother's dying words to me would be, "You can't spell." And so it came to pass. Despite all the suicide attempts, she lived into her late eighties and was finally dying in a nursing home. I went to visit her as she lay curled up in bed, almost comatose. I said, "It's your son, Lou" to which she responded, as she gradually roused herself, "I have another son?" I replied, "Yes, you have two sons, Ivan and me." This brought her fully awake, she rose to a sitting position, and said, "Ivan and *I*." And these were her last words to me, correcting my grammar (and getting it wrong). I make a joke out of it, but the last twenty years of her life, after my father's death, were a long slow decline into immobility, not really funny, though humor can ease the pain.

Just as I broke free of my basketball block in my freshman year of college, I overcame my uneven academic performance when I began graduate school in psychology. I got married at age twenty-one and, by thirty-one, had three children: two daughters and a son. After more than thirty years, with the kids grown and on their own, I felt that the marriage was troubled in ways that could not be resolved and got a divorce. This naturally set off distressing reactions through the whole family and was the most painful emotional experience of my adult life. Fortunately, I remarried and my new wife Barbara and I have been very happy for the last twenty-five years. The one redeeming aspect of this emotional upheaval was a deeper understanding of patients going through marital turmoil or divorce. The divorce had reverberations with those few patients who found out about it. For example, "Josh" said he heard that a psychoanalyst in Los Angeles named Lou Breger had gotten divorced but he thought it must have been another analyst with that name—there isn't another one in the whole country—showing his need to maintain an idealized image of me.

To sum up the way my childhood affected the kind of psychotherapist I became, I would say that the early love left me with a base of security that allowed me to overcome the various unconscious inhibitions and conflicts that arose later. I always believed that loving relationships were possible, which was conveyed to my patients, both between us, and in my belief that they could achieve this form of happiness in their lives. While the very sensitive little boy—reactive to any hint of criticism—was buried by adolescence, it lived on underground and could be safely present when working with patients. This accounts for why being a nonjudgmental, empathic listener always came easily to me. I was also not materialistic, not that interested in amassing wealth or possessions, but oriented toward meaningful work and creative accomplishments, which, again, were communicated to my patients as worthwhile goals. It also led me to see a number of them for low fees. My family's political radicalism led me to question received doctrines and find my own way, which will become apparent when reviewing my career as a psychologist.

Through the course of my life, I learned a good deal from a variety of actual experiences—interacting with and observing my kids as they grew up, my own analysis, the marriage and divorce, illnesses—which informed my understanding of patients as they described similar events. Finally, there was an element of luck during the years I came of age. I was too young for the Korean War and too old for Vietnam. When I received my doctorate, universities were expanding and good jobs available; and the economy was sound through the years when I was earning a living.

On one occasion, when I was established in my career, a group of psychoanalyst colleagues and I were chatting informally when it turned out that all six of us had depressed mothers. It was clear that this had much to do with our choice to become therapists. Without necessarily knowing it, we were trying to cure our mother's sorrow by curing our patients. With all the neuroses in my family, along with my own unconscious conflicts, it was natural that I was drawn to Freud, who I first read as an undergraduate. Freud's masterful prose and his explanations of neuroses and unconscious motivation were quite captivating. His ideas held out the promise of understanding the disturbance in my family. With a father whom I saw as a failure, Freud, whose genius was accepted by many in the 1950s, became a new ideal. I took up training in clinical psychology with the goal of becoming a therapist, and from the very beginning, doing psychotherapy just seemed like what I was cut out for; it felt natural. Here, I could be immersed in relationships where the goal was deep and lasting psychological healing, as well as openness and emotional honesty.

6

Learning the Ropes

In order to understand, it is immensely important for the person who understands to be located outside the object of his or her creative understanding—in time, in space, in culture. For one cannot ever really see one's own exterior and comprehend it as a whole, and no mirrors or photographs can help; our real exterior can be seen and understood only by other people, because they are located outside us in space, and because they are others.

—Mikhail Bakhtin

I received my Ph.D. in clinical psychology from The Ohio State University in 1961 at a time when the professed ideal was the "tripartite model"; we were encouraged to become a combination clinician-researcher-teacher, a demanding goal, and one that did not particularly appeal to me since I was mainly interested in psychotherapy. Somewhat to my surprise, I seem to have fulfilled the requirement despite my reservations.

While I was drawn to Freud's writings, and was strongly influenced by his ideas, in my second year of graduate school I read an article by John Bowlby—one of the first of what would become attachment theory—which emphasized human relationships of attachment, separation, and loss. Because of my undergraduate appreciation of Darwin, Bowlby's ideas immediately struck me as profound, despite rebuttals by Anna Freud and other psychoanalysts. Bowlby's work, and its later elaborations, has always remained central to my thinking; I have been alert to the crucial role of separations, losses, and the absence of secure relationships as major sources of anxiety and depression.[1] This is illustrated by many of the cases described earlier: Judith, whose mother preferred her sister; Scott, with his guilt-inducing, depressed mother; Emily, who lost her mother's attention when her brother and sister were born; Andrew, whose suicidal depression was set off by his wife's leaving him; Lark, whose mother never gave her the love she needed; and Nino, who, in his forties, was still struggling with the loss of his first love at age eighteen. It was not that these individuals didn't have other conflicts—including guilt, inferiority feelings, sexual acting out, eating disorders—but secure and insecure attachments were at the core of their struggles. Bowlby's ideas also helped explain my own mother's depression, which arose from never having had a secure and loving maternal attachment when she was a child.

After receiving my Ph.D., I took a teaching position at the University of Oregon in Eugene, did research, and saw patients in psychotherapy at our training clinic. The two best known psychologists during those years were Carl Rogers, with his "client centered" school of counseling, and behaviorism, with B. F. Skinner its best known proponent. Neither of these approaches appealed to me; they seemed too simple, too narrow in their foci—Rogers, for example, had no theory of child development—though, looking back, I am much more sympathetic to his work since he, along with his students, did research on the counseling methods they practiced.[2] Behavior therapy, the treatment associated with behaviorism, claimed to be based on the "scientific" findings of learning theory, but my colleague Jim McGaugh—whose research was in learning and memory—and I had questions about these scientific pretensions, read all the available literature, and found that the learning theory they were using was biased, out of date, and did not support their claims. Central was the fact that the actions of human beings, and other animals as well, cannot be explained by simple theories of stimulus and response or rewards and punishments; people have minds, thoughts, plans—called "cognitive maps" in the learning theory literature of the day—and all these needed to be attended to, especially when one is trying to explain disturbed personality and its treatment. We coauthored an article in 1965, reviewing this evidence, and our ideas played an important role in exposing the inadequacies of behavior therapy and pushing it in the direction of a cognitive-behavioral approach. It was my first major publication and was reprinted in a number of books.

I found Freud's complex writings much more to my liking than either Rogers or behaviorism, since they explored unconscious motivation, dreams, case material, child development, transference, and much more. I taught the graduate seminars in psychoanalysis and practiced a version of psychoanalytic therapy. I say "version" since Eugene Oregon was quite isolated; there wasn't a psychoanalyst you could spit on within a hundred miles, so the therapy I did was very much self-taught. Nor was there anyone for me to see in personal therapy or analysis at that time, though I was too emotionally controlled in any case, being very much a do-it-yourself guy. So I was psychoanalytic in my teaching, research, and writing, which allowed me to continue to admire Freud, unaffected by contact with any actual psychoanalysts.

I was not uncritical of psychoanalytic theory, however, and studied dreaming using the relatively new methods for monitoring Rapid Eye Movement (REM) sleep through the night. Waking subjects out of REM sleep and getting their dream reports was a method akin to using a newly discovered microscope; here was a technique that allowed us to gather dream reports—as many as six per night—under a variety of conditions. My colleagues and I reasoned that dream function could best be examined under conditions of arousal or stress, because this would make clear what the day residues were. As one example, we gathered the dreams of subjects in hospitals before and after major surgeries. We felt it was essential that these be interpreted on a case-by-case basis, that we study each person's unique dream "language," and not lump them into a statistical pool. For example, one older man, who had worked most of his life as a logger, dreamt about his vascular surgery with mechanical symbols such as plumbers fixing leaking pipes. For him, the danger of surgery—his condition was, in fact, life threatening—was being in a dependent position, putting himself in the hands of "young fellas"—the surgeons—who might not know how to repair his broken parts. In contrast, an overweight young woman, undergoing surgery for a stomach ulcer, dreamt about being thin and more attractive after her operation and, as a result, becoming more popular with boys. Dreams, we believed, could not be understood without understanding individual meanings such as these.

Freud always considered *The Interpretation of Dreams* his most significant book and I was very taken with it, beginning the REM dream research thinking that I would find confirmation of his ideas. If the theory were not entirely valid, it would be interesting to find out what function dreams did serve. Freud held that dreams, like neurotic symptoms, were the disguised fulfillment of unconscious—primarily sexual—wishes. Our research, published in my monograph *Function of Dreams* and the coauthored book, *The Effect of Stress on Dreams* did not substantiate Freud's theory, though he was correct that dreams were meaningful and could be used as a road—if not "the royal road"—to the emotionally laden, unconscious side of the person. The studies we carried out were consistent with a good deal of evidence gathered by other investigators,[3] evidence which demonstrated that dreams are symbolic-imaginative attempts to come to terms with the emotional issues stirred up during the preceding day and, in addition, that they are frequently suffused with anxiety and a variety of other emotions, including, but not restricted to, sexuality.[4]

The dream research also led me to a critical consideration of Freud's general theories of motivation.[5] I think that this work had two effects on my practice as a therapist. First, the findings made clear that dreams could not be meaningfully understood as the disguised fulfillment of wishes—sexual or otherwise—and I became much more sensitive to their adaptive function: how they were imaginative attempts at the mastery of emotional conflicts. Second, immersing myself in all this dream material, and relating it to the personalities of the dreamers, was like an advanced course in learning a foreign language; I came to feel that I could understand the "language" of dreams with some facility.

I moved to the Langley Porter Institute in 1966 and then was a Visiting Professor at The University of California at Berkeley from 1969 to 1970 and, at both these venues, there was more opportunity for contact with psychoanalysts, Jungian therapists, and others. With my supportive older colleague Ginny Patterson and others, we began a program of time-limited psychotherapy: ten sessions or less.[6] This research involved listening to many tape-recorded examples of the work of trainees and staff members with a wide variety of patients. Follow-up interviews demonstrated that all kinds of people could benefit from therapy—psychoanalytic, behavioral, Jungian—however brief, and that therapists differed greatly in their abilities to work with these patients.

The research also showed that the personal qualities of the therapist were more important to the success of the treatment than their theoretical orientation. Jerome Frank (1961) was one of the earliest to identify the common factors across many forms of psychological healing. It is now well established that there are personal characteristics of therapists that account for the success of therapy derived from many different schools. Ablon and Jones (1998), for example, indicate that cognitive-behavioral therapy is effective when the therapists use analytic psychotherapy methods: that it is the kind of person and the relationship that is most important. Those who follow a CBT manual in a standardized way do not achieve positive results. My patient Alejandro, who saw a CBT therapist after many years of successful work with me, stresses the personal and relational qualities of that therapy and not any behavioral "techniques." A long-term benefit of this psychotherapy research came from my immersion in the clinical material: doing brief therapy myself, supervising students, and listening to and discussing many tape-recorded therapy sessions.

I did most of the writing of my book *From Instinct to Identity: The Development of Personality* at Langley Porter and Berkeley, a work in which I attempted to integrate the ideas of Freud, Bowlby, the Neo-Freudians, Jean Piaget, research findings on nonhuman primates, hunter-gatherer cultures, dreams, and child development. The research and writing of this book solidified my developmental orientation. That is, when listening to patients talk about their childhood experiences, I found it important to attend to the psychological capacities available at the age being described: to imagine myself into the mind of a five- or ten-year-old, or an adolescent. As just one example, "Rory" was a patient who was essentially unwanted and not responded to by his mother. His father was away long hours at work and also not available. What memories he did have from his earliest years were of an atmo-sphere of grayness: a feeling of sadness that was hard to put into words, along with visual images of his mother's back as she moved away from him. These experiences were hard to talk about because they originated at a time before he had language, though they continued throughout the later years of his childhood. His deepest emotional deprivation was prelinguistic, encoded in what is called "procedural"—emotional, bodily—rather than "declarative" or language-based memory. This early extreme emotional deprivation predisposed him to respond to women primarily in terms of their physical characteristics. He was repeatedly drawn to women because of the shape of their bodies and their sexual attractiveness, even when he and they had little in common intellectually or emotionally; in fact, even when they were psychologi-cally disturbed or treated him badly.

Several other writers also influenced my thinking in those days. In addition to the work of Bowlby and child development research, I was taken with Erik Erikson's 1950 book *Childhood and Society*, which, while not presented as a direct challenge to Freud, neverthe-less introduced essential social, cultural, and historical dimensions to psychoanalysis, as well as extending psychological development into the adolescent and adult years. Also important was a 1975 essay by the German ethologist Norbert Bischof—*The Biological Basis of the Incest Taboo*—that stood psychoanalytic instinct theory and the Oedipus complex on their heads.[7] While still strongly taken with Freud's writings, I doubted that sexuality and the Oedipus complex were at the core of every neurosis, including my own, and those of my patients. I should add that, though I was critical of many aspects of psychoanalytic theory, I did not question the belief that the therapy was the best, that it was the path to one's deepest unconscious conflicts, and the only way to really resolve them.

In 1970, I was appointed a Professor in the Humanities and Social Science Division at the *California Institute of Technology* in Pasadena, where my colleagues were faculty members in history, literature, philosophy, anthropology, and economics. I co-taught courses in psychohistory and psychoanalysis and literature, a stimulus for my book *Dostoevsky: The Author as Psychoanalyst.* For many years I have been a teacher at both the undergraduate, graduate, and postgraduate levels. I was never particularly enamored of lecturing and always preferred seminars where I could engage the students in dialogues. This was the teaching version of my relational approach to psychotherapy. At Caltech, a group of us from the different disciplines formed an informal reading and discussion group where we could share ideas about psychoanalysis and related topics. Like the undergraduate teaching, the atmosphere was an open one where we explored different concepts and points of view.

All of this work—the research on dreaming and brief psychotherapy, the critical exploration of drive theory, exposure to the work of Bowlby and others who critiqued and revised psychoanalytic theory, writing the books on personality development and Dostoevsky, and the open discussions with my colleagues at Caltech, led me to think that psychoanalysis was, or should be, an open-minded, scientific field. With a background in scholarship and research, I thought that once things were demonstrated by studies—such as the research on dreaming or mother–infant attachment—or sufficient findings were marshaled from diverse sources, psychoanalysis would drop Freud's theories and methods that did not stand up to the new evidence; that it would change like any other scientific or scholarly field. For example, once it was shown that as many as eighty per cent of stomach ulcers are caused by a particular bacterium—helicobacter pylori—there was an initial period of skepticism, which led to further research. This established the validity of the new theory and physicians began treating their ulcer patients with antibiotics rather than sending them to psychiatrists. My experience with organized psychoanalysis was soon to prove that it did not follow such a path.

7

Looking for the "Pure Gold"

*Little distinction was made between received wisdom and fact. Any
adulteration of existing beliefs—for example, attention to cultural
inputs—was privately felt to be heresy—an adulteration of Freud's
'pure gold'—and publicly dismissed as a resistance to the truth of the
Oedipus complex, the shibboleth—as Freud had put it—on which
psychoanalysis stood or fell.*

—John M. Ross

A few years after joining the faculty at Caltech, I finally became
affiliated with organized psychoanalysis, undergoing training as a
"research candidate" at the Southern California Psychoanalytic Institute: research candidate because the Institute, like all those affiliated
with The American Psychoanalytic Association, still, with a very few
exceptions, restricted training to psychiatrists. This rule, put in place in
America in the years between the two World Wars, though personally
opposed by Freud, was an example of the narrowness of institutional
psychoanalysis. Many of the most creative and original contributors
to the field such as Otto Rank, Erich Fromm, and Erik Erikson would
not have been allowed to become psychoanalysts under this policy.

Training in the Institute had three main components: the personal or training analysis, the supervision of cases in psychoanalytic
treatment—discussed in Chapter 2—and seminars in which we discussed readings. Analysts generally agreed that the personal analysis
was the most significant part of the training, which was certainly the
case with me. I was thirty-nine years old when I began training at
the Southern California Institute and, despite having seen patients
in therapy since I was twenty-four, had never had a single session
of therapy for myself. Talk about emotional constriction! I decided
that, since I was finally entering analysis, I would throw myself into it
wholeheartedly. I came five times a week, lay on the couch, recorded
my dreams and reported them faithfully, and made every effort to associate freely without holding anything back.

My training analyst did not entirely adhere to orthodox methods, and we seemed to have political and social views in common, so we were a good fit, which was lucky for me, since it was almost impossible to change analysts once you began your training. I felt I had at last found a man whom I could admire and idealize, something that had long been missing from my life. Freud also continued to be something of a hero, and I kept a picture of him on the wall of my office.

The four-and-a-half years I spent in the personal psychoanalysis were very helpful and, as I look back, what stands out was my relief at finally being with someone who listened to me, who made an effort to understand me, and where, on at least a few occasions, I was able to let my emotions go, especially to cry—mainly about the sadness of my mother's life—which was something I had not done since I was a young boy. I also remember some of the interpretations as helpful in identifying life patterns of which I was unaware, including the way I "hid my light under a bushel" as my analyst put it, that is, did not sufficiently value my own accomplishments. But it was the relationship itself—being accepted, listened to in a noncritical manner, understood, appreciated, even liked—after revealing what I felt were my most shameful and guilt-ridden secrets—that was most helpful. I also remember one occasion when my analyst let his personal concerns intrude into the treatment, telling me about some troubles he was having with his own children, which I found quite upsetting. Fortunately, he called me at home that evening, apologized for his mistake, and told me he would not charge for that session.

Overall, the training analysis was very helpful in loosening me up emotionally, freeing me from excessive guilt, and helping me realize that, despite my accomplishments and professorship at a prestigious institution, there were ways in which I continued to think of myself as the inadequate person I felt I was as a child and young man. I became much less shy, was able to express myself comfortably, and the old anxiety about telling others what I felt and thought was largely gone. The analysis also helped me to become a better psychotherapist, since I now appreciated, first hand, what it was like to be on the other side of the relationship.

While my own training analysis was a largely positive one, many of the other candidates did not have such helpful experiences. And those at other, more orthodox institutes, were even worse. Jeffrey Masson, in his 1992 book, describes his training analysis at the Toronto Institute with a man who was arbitrary, domineering, and downright insulting at times, all within a system where he, as a candidate, could do nothing about the abuse he was forced to endure. Needless to say, the therapy was not at all beneficial.

I eventually got to know a large number of people who had undergone psychoanalytic treatment, both older members who had their analyses in the heyday of orthodoxy, my fellow candidates in the 1970s, and many others. The results of these treatments were quite variable; my largely positive experience was at the far end of the spectrum while others had much more uneven—if not destructive—results. While some received valuable help, others had a mixed experience, and, for still others, major problematic areas of their lives remained untouched. Then there were those who experienced real damage of two kinds. First, there were obviously harmful treatments where individuals were not helped, were not understood, and where their depression, anxiety, and other problems were not alleviated, as they lay on the couch for years with a largely silent analyst or were subjected to textbook interpretations and told they were resistant if they did not agree. Second, was the damage caused by lost opportunities. I knew a number of people who entered analysis at a time in their lives when they were just embarking on their adult careers and were open to meaningful personal change, only to have this opportunity dashed at the hands of a rigid, insensitive, or downright incompetent analyst.

The third component of Institute training, the seminars, was not at the highest intellectual level. The curriculum was fixed, there were no electives, despite this being a post-postgraduate level of education. And the readings consisted predominantly of Freud's writings and those of his loyal followers. It provided a much more rigid learning experience than the way I taught my undergraduate students. For example, there was just one course over the four years titled "Psychoanalytic Dissidents," in which the work of all the Neo-Freudians and modern thinkers was compressed into eight sessions. When I pointed out the pejorative nature of the term "dissidents" to the instructor, he seemed perplexed. One of the few stimulating seminars consisted of our reading Freud's well-known case studies, as well as a number of articles discussing each case. The candidates made presentations of these cases, and the related literature, and, when I discussed the case of Schreber—a famous psychotic judge who Freud analyzed based on his published Memoirs—I spoke of how his psychosis seemed a result of the severe abuse he had suffered as a child. This was a contrast to Freud's interpretation, which located the cause of Schreber's breakdown in his presumed "latent homosexual impulses." The seminar instructor seemed at a loss of what to make of this alternative explanation. Despite these considerable limitations, the seminars were the place where camaraderie developed with my fellow candidates.

Overall, my experience at the Southern California Psychoanalytic Institute was very uneven. The training analysis was helpful to me personally, but for the most part, the supervision of cases was not. The seminars went into more detail about those of Freud's ideas that were valuable—unconscious motivation, the interpretation of dreams, the model of child development, and the general approach to analytic psychotherapy—though, in all these areas, there were outmoded and invalid ideas mixed in with what was useful.[1] And there were all of the wrong paths taken by Freud, and continued by his orthodox followers: the neglect, if not dismissal, of the significance of trauma and the real experiences of childhood, the belief that homosexuality was a disease in need of psychoanalytic cure, the view of sexuality as a dangerous instinct in need of sublimation, and his views regarding the inferiority of women.[2] As an example of this last point, in her wonderful memoir, Brenda Webster describes her analyses with two well-known classical psychoanalysts—Kurt Eissler and Anna Maenchen—who pushed her into a disastrous marriage since, in their minds, this was all a "normal" woman was suited for. As Webster puts it, "Maenchen subscribed to Freud's theory that having a baby is a woman's way of compensating for her penisless state."

Throughout the five years of my training, I continued to practice therapy, saw the required patients in supervised psychoanalyses, engaged in my personal analysis, read widely in the literature, taught at Caltech, wrote, and, at home, loved, cared for, and observed my three children as they grew up. In all these places, I looked, as objectively as I could, for the various psychoanalytic phenomena that Freud described: by and large I could not find a great many of them. Neurotic conflicts did not arise from anyone's instincts, wishes, and fantasies but from real experiences of trauma, deprivation, loss, abuse, lack of empathy, and the like. There was no psychosexual oral stage, and certainly no "oral sadism," though nursing and sucking were clearly parts of the larger pattern of mother–infant attachment; Harry Harlow's well-known experiments on wire and cloth monkey "mothers" had been published a few years earlier. Young children would display anger, though rarely sadism, when they were frustrated or mistreated. Nor was there a sexualized anal stage, though two-year-old negativism and the early push for autonomy were easy to observe. Oedipal feelings were sometimes apparent but I saw no great Oedipal conflicts—except where parents were sexually inappropriate with their children—nor did my daughters display any penis envy, though my son worked to define his identity as a male, caught between two sisters.[3]

I never agreed with Freud's ideas about women: not just "penis envy" and the "castration complex," but what became the received psychoanalytic view that, unless women were docile wives and mothers, they were neurotic. In several of my cases I was pleased to see women patients pursue careers, sometimes combined with motherhood, while in another—Elizabeth—a successful outcome of her therapy was to set aside her drive for professional accomplishment so she could devote herself to her children when they were small. No one template fits each individual. Nor was I sympathetic to Freud's views about ordinary or working-class people, who he referred to as "the mob" or "the rabble." My own attitude was no doubt influenced by my family's glorification of "the working man." While he published nothing that could be called openly racist, Freud's theories that traced all forms of psychological disturbance to childhood events like the Oedipus complex left no place for the profoundly damaging effects of racial, religious, and other forms of discrimination. Over the years, only a miniscule number of African American and other minorities were trained in psychoanalytic institutes. Interestingly, when the Supreme Court struck down discrimination in schools in its momentous *Brown v. Board of Education* decision, it cited the harmful effects of segregation on children, based on psychological—but not psychoanalytic—research.

I think all these Freudian prejudices passed me by because they were so foreign to my own way of thinking. As I have described, I grew up in a nonreligious, leftist family that valued the working class, was suspicious of the wealthy, was strongly antiracist, and believed in equality between the sexes. My mother was an intelligent college graduate and—while limited by her depression—did enter the world of work. Later, as an adult, I supported my wife's efforts on her jobs and spent a whole summer during graduate school staying home with my six-month-old daughter, which gave me a taste of how difficult what was dismissively labeled "women's work" could be. If I had looked more closely at Freud's ideas about women and the working class—which I eventually did in writing the biography I published in 2000—I would have seen that these beliefs were rooted in his personality. But, at this earlier stage of my career, I assumed these ideas were just relics from the nineteenth century that he had not gotten around to relinquishing.

Early in my practice as a psychoanalytically oriented therapist, I did try out various Freudian interpretations: perhaps this conflict had an Oedipal root, or that woman's ambition and resentment stemmed from her unconscious desire to be a man. I found that these interpretations did little good. Fortunately, my style was always to offer such ideas in a tentative manner, as guesses or hypotheses for the patient to accept or reject. This was, no doubt, the result of both the kind of person I was as well as my university and research background, which led me to value the free expression of ideas and appreciate a wide variety of methods and theories. At least my patients were not subjected to an authoritarian analyst trying to force his version of psychoanalytic "truth" on them.

I graduated from the Southern California Institute in 1979, became a training and supervising analyst five years later, served on various governing committees, and got to know the leaders of the organization, as well as national figures. To become a training analyst one had to submit a minimum of three written reports of one's supervised cases to a committee of the national organization—The American Psychoanalytic Association—and it was generally put about that, to be approved, you faked these reports to some extent. One left out anything that hinted at contemporary or nonorthodox ideas, while emphasizing such things as Oedipal conflicts and transference interpretations. This was another example of the authoritarian control that was so prevalent in organized psychoanalysis, for I cannot imagine any university department allowing hiring, tenure decisions, or promotions to be controlled by a distant, national body.

In the 1980s, a group of analysts at the Southern California Institute became interested in the new self-psychological theories of Heinz Kohut[4]; they were dissatisfied with the effectiveness of classical psychoanalysis, despite their many years of experience. While many of the orthodox members of the Institute disparaged these interests, it was a breath of fresh air in an organization that was a closed system, derogating ideas and research outside of its officially sanctioned channels. Self-psychology moved away from the Freudian focus on sources of pathology within the person, as typified by drive theory, and emphasized the patient's early experiences of lack of emotional attunement at the hands of his or her parents. This led to a form of therapy in which the analyst's empathy and attunement were central.

At this time, a serious conflict developed within the Institute around the admission of nonmedical candidates, as well as between orthodoxy and new approaches such as self-psychology. This eventually motivated me to lead a group of members to break away and found a new training center: The Institute of Contemporary Psychoanalysis (ICP). We structured ICP as a democratic institution where power and authority were shared; the president and the governing board were elected and were representative of different constituencies, including candidates in training. Every graduate could easily become a training and supervising analyst. Psychoanalysis has always existed outside of universities and not been subjected to the pluralism and openness to different ideas that, at least as ideals, characterize academic life. At ICP we attempted to bring these principles back into the training program. In addition, we would not be a part of any national organization that constrained our freedom. The new Institute taught self-psychology, relational approaches, attachment theory, intersubjectivity, Freud, infant and developmental research, and offered a number of electives, including those initiated by the candidates. We gave up the old, rigid rules: the couch, silence, abstinence, fixed frequency of sessions, and the like. We also abandoned the criteria of "analyzability" and a wide array of patients were treated as supervised cases, the great majority successfully.

Quitting all the official psychoanalytic organizations and helping to found ICP was the most significant version of a pattern seen earlier in my life when I led mini-democratic revolutions at the University of Oregon and Langley Porter[5]: a legacy of the political ideals I grew up with. Once ICP was firmly established, I turned to writing a biography of Freud. While I had become profoundly disillusioned with organized psychoanalysis, and had long been critical of much of psychoanalytic theory, I still idealized Freud as a person, believing, for example, that the problems with his sexual instinct theory or his ideas about women were due to the lingering influence of ideas from the nineteenth century. Freud, the man, had been understood by most of his biographers in terms of the heroic legend he created. The two biographies I wrote in 2000 and 2009 drew on new theories, his correspondence, accounts provided by patients who had been in analysis with him, and other sources.[6]

One can know something and not know it at the same time, and this is how it was with my feelings about Freud. My view of him and his theories gradually evolved as I researched and wrote the first biography, with very significant creative contributions from my wife Barbara, a historian. It was finally time for the blinders to drop from my eyes, to give up my idealization of Freud, to see him as a flawed human being, as we all are. I came to recognize that the real deficiencies in psychoanalysis had their origins in the kind of person he was: brilliant and creative, a masterful writer, someone who created a theory that drew together a number of crucial ideas and observations and developed a method of treatment from which many later forms of psychotherapy grew. Many of his ideas are still valuable: the model of child development, transference, and the meaningful nature of dreams, among others. But he was also a man who craved heroic stature above all else, was intolerant of the ideas of others, reacted with hatred to those who disagreed with him, and was deeply authoritarian.

8

Patients Speak

Good therapy is like acting—when you need to, you can access the feeling more easily than other people, and it is in that catharsis, that the healing can happen.

—Leo

Usually, when psychotherapy ends, the therapist says goodbye and rarely knows what happens in the years that follow. If the treatment went well, were the gains permanent? Did the patient's symptoms and problems come back or was there further progress? Sometimes there is continuing contact and one can answer these questions, but many times not. One impetus for my contacting patients I had seen years before was to ask them to answer such questions in their own words. Classical psychoanalysts speak of "termination" and being "fully ana-lyzed" as if the patient is someone with an infection which can be cured and nothing further need be done, rather than an individual with a life that goes on, with all its ups and downs, twists and turns. In earlier chapters, I have described the treatment of a number of patients in which it was clear that the gains they made in their psychotherapy were lasting and even, in some cases, led to further emotional development in the succeeding years. Here I will present a number of additional cases, organized in terms of the major factors that were central to the success of their psychotherapies.

A New Relationship

"Christine" was an intelligent, well-educated woman in her early thirties whom I saw for almost twenty years, at first four times a week, tapering down to once a week, ending in 2004. While settled in a rela-tively happy marriage, she was depressed and quite unclear where her life was heading. Motherhood was ruled out; she was adamant that she never wanted to have children, which I never saw as a symptom or sign of neurosis, as an orthodox Freudian might have. She was the only child of an extremely demanding, difficult mother; her parents had divorced when she was six and there had been minimal contact with her father thereafter. She titled her response to my question about her therapy: "20 years of talking, obviously I needed someone to listen." She went on to describe how her mother never believed her and if I ever seemed "bored" it would have "crushed her" but, almost always, I was genuinely interested, which I was.

Christine's description of the most important thing she got from therapy was that "I no longer hated myself...I only got to like myself because I finally felt that YOU liked me." An example from the final period of her therapy gives a clear illustration of this:

> *You were in hospital, in intensive care, on strong painkillers. I was told it was ok to call to speak to you...when I got you on the phone, you sounded genuinely happy to hear my voice. I thought well he is not in his analytic stance now...he is lying there on morphine, for God's sake, he could not fake that tone in his voice.*

What turned Christine from a drifting and self-hating young woman into someone who liked and valued herself, and who began a career as a psychotherapist where her talents flowered, was the experience of a new relationship that countered and undid the damage caused by her mother. Where her mother endlessly criticized and tried to force her to be what she wanted—never listened, never saw things from Christine's point of view—I did the opposite: accepted and liked her, and did not demand that she comply with any agenda of mine. As an aside, one of her minor symptoms was that she could not drive onto freeway ramps because there was a sign that said, "Merge," an interesting symbolic version of her need to protect herself from her mother's attempts to take over her personality. She figured out the meaning of this herself and the symptom went away after several years. If I had pushed her to talk about the transference—an absolute requirement of classical psychoanalysis—I would have been a new version of her mother, trying to make her do what I wanted.

"Josh" was a psychologist in his early thirties who I saw in a training analysis for six years, four times a week, ending in 1989. He came from a large family in which there was a good deal of violence and abuse—both physical and emotional—from his mother, father and older brother. In addition, he was involved in a serious car accident around the age of eight that left him in a body cast for close to a year. Not surprisingly, he became a therapist specializing in the treatment of trauma.

I found my treatment with you revolutionary in terms of helping me create the life I had hoped for. What I felt was most helpful was that I felt truly loved by you. I had never had that from a male authority figure. So much of my childhood I felt like I would make my father happy if I died. He told me many times that he would have been much happier if I and my siblings were never born. Your love was the antidote and the opposite of what I experienced in my childhood. I felt you were very giving to me in terms of time, effort, emotion, and finances in terms of a reduced fee. All of these were very concrete examples of my worth and value to you. I felt you were very interested in my activities, my growth, and in my thoughts. Your dependability and willingness to listen, even sometimes, look inside for problems you had which might interfere with our relationship, was impressive.

I should add that I never said "I love you" or "I like you" to Josh—not because analytic rules prohibited this, with some patients it might be just what was needed—though I felt real affection for him as the analysis progressed. His sense of being loved is what he took from the many different interactions that made up our work together. As with Christine, actions spoke louder than words.

"Ruth" was a therapist in her forties who had suffered moderate to severe depression since adolescence. She describes her analysis—three times a week for eight years, sitting face-to-face, ending in 2003—with me as follows:

For the first time, I had the experience of being listened to by someone who I felt liked me, cared about me, and wanted to know me...We had the same sense of humor...we shared values; political, moral, social... I could swear like a sailor and feel comfortable doing it. I could be myself...You were able to tolerate my incessant whining and depressive complaining. I don't know how you did it. I was such a downer. I think that allowed me to tolerate it in myself...I felt I would be protected... You only wanted the best for me. I guess this was a parental experience I had not had before; not from either my mother or my father... All in all, you provided me with an experience that somehow has enabled me to have a pretty good sense of myself. I carry you around with me always...I like myself, and that's not such a bad thing!

"Isabella" was an intelligent young woman, pursuing a graduate degree in psychology, who I saw for four years, mainly three times a week, ending in 1992. She suffered from anxiety and low self-confidence, though she functioned at a high level in school.

I've been thinking about your query. When I think of the work, what comes to mind as most important has to do with "acceptance." I think this was communicated in many ways—by what you said and did not say, but also more generally by your relaxed demeanor. Something important was communicated in your sense of ease, in the tone of your voice and even a certain ease in the way you held yourself. Your unflappability seems key. And so, by seeming not to be anxious yourself about anything I brought up, even if it did seem to concern you directly, I felt at ease fully to explore my thoughts and express my feelings.

I recall that you didn't seem to feel anxious when I would put you on the spot, challenge you to come up with an interpretation, or invite you to show off your theoretical understanding. So your confidence in the process, your trust in yourself and myself, was comforting.

Next, I think of "generosity." The times you understood my point of view, even when I was pretty sure it wouldn't be your point of view, were meaningful. For example, when I would report my reactions to people we knew in common—other therapists & acquaintances—I was impressed that your relationships to these people did not color your ability to understand my experiences. This seemed to be part of the lesson that it was OK—more than OK—to be me.

As I write this, I realize that you being you was integral to the therapy—you being at ease, comfortable—just as me being me was. Perhaps the word I'm looking for is "authenticity": yours and mine.

"Trust" would be another key concept. I could trust you not to be nutty, vindictive, abusive, exploitative. The trust evolved in the context of the therapeutic frame, the maintenance of boundaries, etc.

It was important that you did not pathologize, seem perturbed, try to fix, or in any way get upset.

I've been asking myself what didn't work in the treatment, and I can't come up with much. Really. While it's possible I don't want to come up with anything negative for fear of not being able to process it, work it through, etc. I really don't feel anything was left amiss. So thank you.

Summing up the successful therapeutic experiences of these four, as well as a number of the patients discussed earlier, it is clear how vital it was that they knew I genuinely liked them and, because of this, could like themselves. Their self-hatred, unhappiness, poor self-esteem, depression, and anxiety had different origins. Judith was largely neglected as a child, as was Lark; Scott subjected to his mother's guilt-inducing attacks, which was also the case with Nino. Christine's intrusive mother wanted to take her over and never recognized her as a separate person; while Josh's father wished he had never been born. Ruth was lost as a middle child with a seriously depressed mother and a father who was busy escaping from his wife into affairs with other women. Isabella suffered the early deaths of both parents, and Andrew went through a very difficult, isolated childhood: his father killed himself and his mother seemed oblivious of his existence. While they had these very different family backgrounds, each had a new experience with me that countered and undid the damage caused by their parents. They had versions of what Franz Alexander, one of many psychoanalysts expelled from the orthodox movement for heretical ideas, called a "corrective emotional experience."[1]

Many of these patients comment on my "humanness" and "humanity," my not doing what they expected from a psychoanalyst, my being open and personal. All these deviations from "the rules" took on special meaning because they were aware of what those rules were; thus, not abiding by them gave my relaxed and natural reactions special significance. For some I had the aura of "a real psychoanalyst," which led them to idealize me and gave special force to what appeared to them as my deviating from the expected framework. To come at it another way, if a patient sees a therapist once or twice and is told "I really like you" or "you're a terrific person" it would probably have little effect. But if they come to feel liked and appreciated in an analytic setting, after several years of increasingly open self-revelation—after baring shameful deeds, secrets, and fantasies—by someone they expect to be objective and circumspect, the impact is much more powerful. Being a relatively informal person, not concerned with status and position, came through to many of them as "humaneness," a demeanor that allowed them to feel relaxed and open in turn. As a final point, it is interesting that what I think of as my emotional over-control and workaholism, many of them experienced as steadiness, reliability, and unflappability.

The Ideal and the Flawed

"Leo"—a pseudonym he chose because of his admiration of James Joyce's *Ulysses* and its hero Leo Bloom—was a brilliant writer who suffered bouts of anxiety that took somatic forms along with considerable unwarranted guilt and fear such as his belief that the police or FBI would mistake him for a criminal. Some of this could have been due to his highly sensitive and imaginative nature: reactions that are common in creative individuals. His father was both encouraging of his talents and competitive—not unlike the competitiveness that both my parents displayed toward me—so that, early in his career, Leo felt he had to do his writing in secret. I saw him for eight years, three times a week, until 1997, and then for varying periods until 2004. He first came to see me around the age of thirty, having spent a good part of his twenties in treatment with a classical Freudian and getting very little out of the experience. Early in his treatment, we spent considerable time undoing the ill effects of this previous analysis, with him venting his anger, particularly at the years of his life that were wasted in that endeavor. Here is his account:

> *Therapy is a wonderful, flawed, limited, potentially limitless process like life itself. None of us lives an ideal existence and none of us becomes "cured" as Freud promised—or as he organized his somewhat rigid thinking. But it gives us wonderful tools to glimpse beneath the surface layer of our existence, to pause, to check ourselves, to understand our behavior, to grow from the insight and experience—and repeat them all again, hopefully with more understanding.*
>
> *We had a WONDERFUL dialogue, you and I, for so long that was so enriching. We saw the world epically. We saw the ironies and shared them. Your great strength as a therapist was that you always showed your humanity, and, in so doing, humanized the process. You demystified yourself and thus analysis. That alone is a gift to someone, Lou. And it allowed me to see my own flaws and vulnerabilities as normal...in not trying to become a god, a savior, a substitute father, or a pillar of strength and certainty to supplant my own confusion, you were ultimately true to your convictions about treatment. It is up to us to live our lives—not up to you. I loved every moment of our journey together.*

What was most therapeutic in Leo's analysis, as in a number of the other therapies, was our living relationship with all its benefits and flaws. For him, especially, it was a relationship with a man that corrected what he had gone through with both his father and his previous psychoanalyst, who acted like omniscient authorities. The fact that I was imperfect, not narcissistic, and didn't come across as an all-knowing authority, allowed him to accept his own shortcomings and vulnerabilities.

The Analysis of a Gay Man

Until the last few decades, homosexuality was a powerful taboo in American society and many individuals were forced to hide their sexual orientation and suffer in silence. Calvin Trillin's revealing elegy, *Remembering Denny*, presents a picture of his college classmate whose very promising life was destroyed because he could not openly reveal his homosexuality. While I, like Trillin and Denny, came of age in the 1950s when these prejudices were still strong, by the time I began practicing psychotherapy, the gay liberation movement, and other developments, had begun to overturn them—though there remain strong antigay feelings in our society—and I did not think of homosexuality as a disease in need of treatment. Nevertheless, I was not entirely free of bias, as the following report of a gay patient will reveal.

"Oliver" was a twenty-four-year-old, openly gay, graduate student in clinical psychology when he began his analysis. I saw him for four years, four times a week, ending in 1987. Here is his account of the therapy:

> *Reflecting on this experience with you so long ago makes me smile, like remembering a journey I took with someone...As a budding psychologist during that process I was also studying what was happening to me and with you...I did not seek a permanent mentor relationship. I had "neuroses" I wanted to cure...For several years after my analysis I would express that there was a clear demarcation between my life before and after analysis. It had that big of an impact on me.*

> *One very simple yet profound effect you had on me was that of role model. I patterned my clinical behavior on you, or my positive projections of you. Whether or not there is a causal relationship is not for me to say, but I have been very successful in my career. You served as a vital container to me, a witness of my life. One description of you I have continually used throughout the subsequent years in describing my experience of analysis is that "you stayed out of my way." I think of the medical maxim: "Do no harm." You did a terrific job of that, for which I have always been grateful...*

> *I mentioned your biases. They came across to me this way: as much as you seemed interested in my dreams, you managed to get me to do all of the interpreting. You were positively biased towards my autonomy and independence: you didn't want to be the all-knowing analyst. This was optimally frustrating and helped me depend upon myself. I remember complaining about it but benefiting in the long run that you did not capitulate to my desire for you to do the interpreting. A negative bias you seemed to have was against the relationship I had with my boyfriend. I don't remember you saying anything at all about him, other than one negative reference about "his limitations." That*

phrase, being the only thing out of your mouth about him, certainly stuck in my mind, and may have supported my inevitable decision to leave him. In retrospect, I regret that you were not more pro-relationship. Had you been encouraging of my relationship, I might have tried harder to stay with him in spite of MY limitations. That did not help me. I remember wondering if this aspect in my analysis came out of your countertransference with your problems in your marriage [being a very intuitive fellow, he must have picked up on problems in my marriage since I did not talk about them] *or from your homophobia. The second bias came as my sexuality was being expressed—or acted out—I'm not sure now, and I said something about wanting you to come lie on the couch next to me. You spoke of a limit, something that intoned you wanted me to keep on talking—revealing a spike in anxiety and your homophobia.*

A few more issues come to mind...You were very encouraging about my graduate education and outright congratulatory as I passed my Ph.D. oral defense and license exams. That felt great...You seemed very interested in my clinical work. I was seeing schizophrenics and... I imagined you had not been as deeply exposed to that clinical population and I enjoyed and benefited from what felt like your interest. It also helped balance my perceived inequity with you as I might have known more than you in that department professionally...You seemed in the dark about the gay culture, yet I didn't get too much homophobia from you except the times I mentioned above. That was okay with me as I didn't mind explaining things I perceived you not being exposed to. Again, another small factor where I knew more. That just felt buoyant and rewarding...You seemed to have pride in and enjoyment of your heterosexuality [he later explained that he picked this up from the way I looked at an attractive woman who we passed in the hallway and not from anything I said.] *That was interesting to me and didn't get in my way, but stands out as a dynamic between a hetero analyst and homo analysand. Sexuality was a big deal to me, so there's no surprise of its inclusion in our journey. It was also an aspect of your healthy role modeling.*

Did analysis cure me of all ailments? No. Did it help me, absolutely yes. Would I recommend analysis to someone with the means to afford it, again absolutely yes. Would I caution them about the sanity/integrity/competence of their analyst, yes again. I'm grateful that at least in the analysis room, you were competent, sane, and a normal, decent human being.

It is now more than twenty years since the completion of Oliver's analysis and it was clearly successful; he is happy and a talented psychotherapist, some of which he credits to modeling himself on how I worked with him. Oliver was a basically healthy young man, there was not a great deal of anxiety or depression; he sailed through graduate school with few blocks or conflicts. The major issues we worked on were his finding a satisfying relationship and the traumas of his childhood, especially the unexpected death of his father when he was thirteen and the equally unexpected death of his older brother at age twenty. Much of what he describes as helpful falls under the heading of a "new relational experience": my enthusiasm about his success in his profession, my interest in his work, and the times he could teach me things and feel he was my equal. He recalls no specific interpretations that I made but, rather, speaks of how I aided his independence by letting him work out insights on his own.

His core identity as a gay man was never something he questioned or wanted to work on in the analysis, and I saw it the same way though, as he points out, there were a few instances of my "homophobia." He knew he was gay from at least the age of ten and was fortunate to grow up at a time when his sexual orientation was far more acceptable than in previous years.

Therapeutic Mistakes and Repair

No matter how aware and empathic a therapist is he or she is bound to make mistakes; the key to good therapy is to honestly admit them and attempt to repair the damage. Several patients will illustrate this point.

Oliver reports my mistakes and how they were dealt with:

> I can only remember a couple "mistakes" you made. They in and of themselves are not an issue for me; it was how you handled them that was so helpful to me. One time you crossed by the waiting room door...and had a "stop nagging me" tone in your voice as you said "I'll be right there." I nailed you on that tone, accusing you of irritation with your wife that did not belong to me. Your reply was simply "you're right." Done. I was impressed and better understood... The second one came as my sexuality was being expressed...and I said something about wanting you to come lie on the couch next to me. You spoke of a limit, something that intoned you wanted me to keep on talking—revealing a spike in anxiety and your homophobia. When I nailed you on it, and accused you of being homophobic...you simply and once again just agreed. No explanations, no defensiveness, just acknowledgment. That had a fantastic and palliative effect on me. Again, you were just "getting out of my way."

"Alejandro" was a brilliant writer, and his treatment was long and complex. We met four times a week for four years, with him lying on the couch, until 1988, and then for various periods, once a week, for a number of years thereafter. His first response to my query about our therapy was:

> The work we did in the 1980s saved my life. I was a mess when I started therapy, a few months off a year and a half of cocaine. I had to ask my parents for money. I told my father, "I'm sick" and he believed me. Within a few years my life was better, but I stayed with the therapy, on and off, until your retirement…I demanded to lie on the couch like a Viennese neurotic. In our first session you even said it, "It's clear you're neurotic." I wouldn't let you talk much for the first month or so, since I was so unhappy and fearful of any breach of whatever perfection I wanted from you. You made a great mistake once, casually referring to your friendship with someone I thought would save my dying career. You had a picture at the foot of the couch I kicked it and the glass in the frame broke and I ran out of the office. Later, I called you from a gas station phone and ranted about your violation of the rules, and a raving lunatic from one of the rooming houses on the street mocked me, and that kind of settled me quickly, and I came back to therapy, and that's when we really began.

I, too, recall this incident and recognized my mistake in mentioning that I knew the person he was talking about and, when he returned, apologized. In this early stage of the treatment, Alejandro needed me to fit the image of a "real psychoanalyst," not, as he put it, "some new age flake."

Both Josh and Ruth mention my bringing in concerns of my own that put them in uncomfortable positions. Josh said, "If there were any problems it really involved aspects of Institute politics invading our relationship. There were moments where I believed these compromised my safe space in the analysis." Likewise, Ruth said, "The only thing that caused me some hesitation was that sometimes we would disagree about ICP politics and I just didn't want to bring it into treatment. So, I tried to avoid it. I didn't want to feel like I had to accommodate to your point of view." I know that Josh confronted me with this problem and that I apologized and stopped doing it while Ruth did not bring it up, though I would have handled it the same way if she had.

"MaryAnn," a woman who always went her own way—creative, artistic, caring for all life forms—saw me in an ICP training analysis for eight years, four times a week, ending in 1998. Her response to my question about her analysis was complex; I will pull out her comments that relate to mistakes:

> *I think of the experience as a kind of woven or baked whole. Something organic between the two of us, muddling along as best we could, meeting up a lot, sometimes not, learning to put things together in new ways so understanding could be deepened...So I think, for now at least, of my analysis with you as a terribly important experience in honesty and empathy. I don't want to discount how the space you made for you and me to hear me had a huge and positive impact on my intellectual life and practice of psychology. Since my analysis I have many times experienced that people don't understand me.* [Because we were so different, I was not sure I always understood her.] *It is less painful and even less important now. Maybe that is acceptance? Little mistakes, even big ones along the way, seem of little impact now. In everything—analysis included—there is muddle. It isn't a mistake so much as part of the process, even if at the time it felt bad, it's a necessary part of coming into consciousness. Not that we muddled much, I don't think we did. Just enough.*

Self-Disclosure

While orthodox psychoanalysis strictly prohibits the analyst's revealing anything about his or her personal life, I have found that, when done in ways that serve the patient's interests, it can greatly facilitate therapeutic progress. Here, as elsewhere, my guide is what I would call the new fundamental rule: whatever one does as a therapist must be for the patient's needs and not one's own. (Freud's "fundamental rule" was that the patient must free associate, say everything that comes to mind, even if it seems trivial or unimportant). Several examples will illustrate this.

Work with Rory will illustrate how one cannot predict in advance— and especially from theory or rules—the meaning of self-disclosures. Rory was working on a project that related to the book on Dostoevsky that I had written some years ago and, when this came up in his analysis, I offered to give him a copy, but with some trepidation; I was afraid that I might be showing off or that he would feel inadequate in relation to me. Contrary to my fear, he had a very positive reaction:

> *My reaction to your book had to do with the experience of having such a supportive, completely accepting figure, who also is so accomplished*

and sharp. I thought of the head of the office where I did my fellowship as an example of an alternative figure, one who is accepting and even admiring of me, but who also is inept and incompetent. There was also the feature of how I seemed to have such a natural feeling about how to flatter his vulnerabilities—always stroking him, letting him know that he was in charge, essentially engaging with him in the game of pretend that he knew what he was doing—and how this allowed me to manage him much better than most people.

Another example comes from "Seth," an overly conscientious and guilt-ridden man who suffered moderate depression for many years, set off by the death of his mother when he was in mid-childhood. I saw him for seven years, ending in 1997. Seth's therapy began well, and he decided to increase his sessions from once to twice a week. Unfortunately, when he appeared for his newly scheduled second session, I wasn't there. I had forgotten the appointment and not written it in my calendar. He was very disheartened by my failure and thought of quitting therapy until I explained to him that I was preoccupied with a matter in my personal life, describing as much about it as seemed appropriate, and this was greatly relieving to him. The missed appointment was my fault and not his and I owned up to it. He reported that his trust in me was solidified by my openness and that his therapy began in earnest from that point on. As he summed up his therapy later,

> *Thank you for being a man I can idealize for being real. Sharing the new book* [to have him check this account, I sent him the whole manuscript of the book, which he read] *gave me a greater appreciation of the time we spent together. Reading the various experiences stimulated even greater understanding of self and other. My experience with you was beyond corrective.*

Scott reported:

> *It helped that you shared stuff from your own life experience and made me feel less intimidated in the relationship. "Hey, this guy's got problems too." The fact that you succeeded in your life problems didn't hurt either.*

These examples from the cases of Rory, Seth, and Scott—as well as Oliver—show the therapeutic effects of an open, honest response; they demonstrate how actions that might seem to be self-serving or for the therapist's needs, were actually illuminating and helpful for these individuals. Learning about me as a person was a part of the therapy with a number of other patients, but it was typically something that occurred late in the work. An element of genuine friendship came to characterize the relationships with a great many of them, though they made clear that this was not what they wanted at earlier stages of the treatment.

Humor

Must I talk about those vaginas...or can I say whatever I want?
—Alejandro

An office mate had installed some photographs in the hall of my office building, close-ups of purple orchids. I picked up Alejandro in the waiting room and he strode to my office in his usual determined way, barely glancing at the photos. He came in, sat down, and said, "Must I talk about those vaginas...or can I say whatever I want?" We both cracked up laughing. The remark revealed his ability to play with sexual symbols, the idea that I—like the good Freudian he knew I wasn't—had put up the pictures to deliberately push his thoughts toward sex, the question of whether he had to comply with this manipulation, and, finally, how we could both laugh in a relaxed manner and felt no need to "analyze" his remark in terms of its meaning. His remark, and our way of dealing with it, condenses much of the difference between the old and new forms of psychoanalysis.

The sharing of humor is part of the overall, relaxed relationship so central to effective analytic therapy. Judith said, "You always had a good sense of humor—which was very important, because I often couched my emotions in humor." Christine recalled a time when my fancy Eames chair broke and I fell on my ass during a session, vainly holding my coffee cup in the air, and we both cracked up laughing. She commented:

> *That you allowed me to laugh for the ENTIRE session...I recall that I was unable to say a single word, and left screaming with laughter. Very undefensive of you to take that so well. What was so funny was that I had come straight from my gynecologist, walked into your office, hit the couch and announced that my tests showed that I was NOT in menopause and that was when you hit the floor...it was not just the fall, but the timing and the context. And then I looked at the bookcase and saw a book by Kafka and there you were like a beetle lying on its*

back with its legs in the air...You were human in your response, I can only imagine how some other analysts might have reacted.

This incident is forever engraved in both of our memories as a special moment of shared laughter.

Leo had a very creative sense of humor and, in one session, got to musing about the movie *Dances with Wolves*, where the Native Americans are all given names based on defining incidents in their lives: *Wind in His Hair, Stands with a Fist*, and *Dances with Wolves* himself. So what was my name? *Nods a Lot.* Very funny, as well as very fitting, I thought. I should put it on my business card.

"Monk," a former patient who does not appear in this book, suffered from a number of severe obsessions and compulsive rituals. One of these consisted in keeping notebooks in which he recorded, in a private code, many of his compulsive activities. For example: "check the gas on the stove" would be recorded as "ctgots," followed by a series of dots, indicating how many times he did this. He was a television journalist who had been working on a story that involved the FBI and was flown to Bureau headquarters in Washington, DC, where he was taken on a tour by one of the agents who was very curious about the notebooks that Monk carried everywhere and that he would not part with. The agent finally managed to get them away from him and no doubt sent them to their decoding experts to see what sinister information they contained. Monk and I laughed wondering what they made of his secret codes: what could "ctgots dot, dot, dot," possibly mean, and what threat to national security did it pose?

Catharsis

A crucial aspect of the relationship is the creation of a climate of safety where the patient feels free to express all sides of him or herself, including the most intense emotions: sadness, despair, depression, anger, fear, sexual longing, love, and others. Leo described how one of the things he took from our work was the ability to get in touch with his grief:

> *...My dad is dying—finally. And I have cut off from him so much. So as a result of treatment and the available insight, suddenly I was able to let the grief come out. Grief for the things I never got. Grief—undefended—for the things I DID get that were wonderful as a child, but was minimizing to make his death easier. Grief for the shattered*

family that I missed. Grief for the way he turned his back. ...So good therapy is like acting—when you need to, you can access the feeling more easily than other people, and it is in that catharsis, that the healing can happen. I have felt good ever since. And that is a dividend of the years you and I spent together.

"Isaac" was someone I saw for ten years, three and then two times a week, ending in 2003. When we began, he was in his late twenties: a very bright, energetic man who had overcome a physically and emotionally abusive childhood at the hands of his father and step-mother. His biological mother, addicted to drugs, had died when he was nine, and he was devoted to giving his children the love and care he had missed himself. While a great many things were covered in this long therapy, in answer to my question, Isaac chose to comment on the catharsis at the very beginning or our work together.

What stands out as most helpful in our work together is your patience. I probably came to your office 125 times before you really started to talk. And I mean talk at all. That was because that was what I needed. You saw that and let it happen. I needed to let out words, feelings, thoughts, anger, etc. If you didn't give me an opportunity to do this I probably would have exploded in one way or another. You gave me a comfortable place to let out my steam. I felt like I was being heard. But it was my agenda. You didn't have a pre-supposed plan that you learned about and tried to instill upon me. You didn't come into the office saying "today we are going to get you to talk about..." That would not have been a natural unraveling of what I needed to do. You gently led—and allowed—me to go down a healthy path. You had a fluidity in your approach. It wasn't a mold or a particular method that existed but more of a natural flow.

"Socrates" was referred to me by a colleague who was treating his wife who was very unhappy in the marriage and told her therapist that, if her husband didn't become more emotionally available, she would seek a divorce. This was news to him, but he loved her and was willing to give therapy a try. He was an intelligent man in his late twenties with a background in economics and business. He was not only unsophisticated regarding psychotherapy, but had studied experimental psychology as an undergraduate, where "talk therapy," was mocked as "unscientific." I saw him once a week for a little over two years, ending in 2002.

Well...I think the most helpful aspect of our work together is also what I disliked the most. The way I recall it, at first, I didn't really get what it was that I was supposed to be working on or how to go about it. I remember sitting in your chair for long periods having no clue what to do. I spent a lot of time hoping that you would give me some guidance or some framework or context within which to think about things. I mostly remember you just nodding and asking simple questions. I felt that for the expense, I ought to be getting sage wisdom. Instead, I feared sitting in your office for our entire session with simply nothing to say, and then getting no satisfying response once I did say something. That was difficult and made me regularly want to quit our sessions.

It got better once I learned the reason why my wife wanted me to see you, i.e., she was unhappy because I was disengaged and my marriage was failing. It took some real dedication on my part to try to stick with you in order to figure out what was happening to me. I remember not knowing what was "OK" to feel, what was a reasonable reaction, etc.

On the other hand, once the ice broke, the foundation for being able to talk about my feelings really enabled me to work through a tsunami of emotions and changes relatively quickly. More importantly, I was able to do it outside of our sessions and on my own. I later understood that that was why it was important that you not be the all knowing sage that I came to depend on. Those tools kind of changed me in some ways, enabling me to cope with things emotionally versus shutting myself down—as I had grown accustomed to doing.

Clearly, the release of "a tsunami of emotions" stands out for this polite young man who, with a fairly chaotic childhood, had learned to bury most of his feelings. It is also interesting that, once the dam broke, he was able to carry on the process outside of therapy. Socrates and his wife have remained happily married, and the family has grown with the birth of three children—who I see every year on a Christmas card—in the nine years since the completion of our work.

Insight

Interpretations and insight played a role in many of my cases but one must distinguish the very different ways interpretations are made, and the role of insight, in classical and contemporary forms of analysis. At its most extreme, the classical analyst acts as the one who knows, the expert who can see into the patient's unconscious, the person whose interpretations will reveal the secret world that drives the neurosis. All the other things that go on in an analysis—the development of a positive relationship, catharsis, the "clearing away" of defenses and resistances—are seen as "preparations" for those telling interpretations that will lead to cure. And such interpretations are often derived from the analyst's theory—think of Nino's and Elizabeth's Kleinian treatments as extreme examples—as opposed to the patient's own experience.

In a contemporary approach, insight is not the be-all and end-all that Freud and his classical followers took it to be. In some of my cases it played an important role, though it was not as central as being listened to and understood; experiencing me and the therapeutic setting as a safe and reliable place; the friendly, caring relationship; attunement, catharsis, and related factors. What is more, I was never an all-knowing analyst who delivered interpretations from on high; insights were worked out collaboratively: "co-constructed," as it is labeled by some modern theorists. In addition, even when an interpretation does not lead to a great illuminating flash, it can be the means by which empathy is conveyed. In other words, from the patient's perspective, an insightful interpretation can be experienced as the analyst really "getting" or understanding them, which can have a greater impact than the unearthing of unconscious material.

Given these caveats, it was still the case that interpretations and insight played some role in many of the cases. The complicated meanings of Gregor's eating and vomiting were understood in terms of a symbolism of the body that represented his emotional relations with his father and mother. Scott and I did a great deal of work exploring how his womanizing was an unconscious means of both obtaining the maternal love he missed and taking revenge on women. Emily and I worked out the meaning of her unsatisfactory relationships with men, which set in motion a process of self-exploration that she continued for many years. And Christine reported that,

> *You didn't push me, didn't analyze every little interaction between us, you tailored the therapy to fit who I was...Something that was extremely important and helpful was getting YOUR take on my experience, re-framing. I guess it takes years to be able to see yourself in another light to see that I was not wrong/cruel/heartless/selfish* [accusations her mother never tired of making].

Josh reported that it was, "Helpful to have my childhood trauma connected to my present behavior and emotional reactions. It made things I did not understand clearer." I have a vivid memory, as I'm sure he does too, of his almost fainting in the delivery room when his wife had to undergo an unexpected caesarian section, an event we were able to connect to the bloody car accident from his childhood.

"Ann" was a research scientist in her forties who I began seeing as her first marriage was breaking up. We met once a week, beginning in 1990, and continue today, once a month by telephone. She suffered from considerable anxiety and also found it difficult to stand up to people who abused and took advantage of her, both in her first marriage and at work. She chose to answer my question about her therapy mainly in terms of insights or things she has come to understand about herself.

1. *Ability to contain anxiety, to isolate what I am actually anxious about and limit my reaction—fine-tune it—to just those circumstances.*

2. *Increased ability to recall past traumatic events, including treatment of me that I experienced as harsh, again with increased ability to separate out treatment that was caused by problems of the other person vs. that caused by my own behavior.*

3. *Increased perception of the other person's anxiety, depression, etc. as a direct cause of their behavior, allowing me to respond more appropriately—less assertively—to a provocation that is rooted not in me, but in the other.*

4. *Increased strength to face loss primarily through actually experiencing partial or threatened loss and surviving it, including your serious, life-threatening experience and [her current husband's] hospitalizations; strength to face significant losses at work and fight against them by standing up for myself...*

5. *Seeing my own over-reaction to bad events in my own life, due to my own determination to not have them flow over to my children especially. This over-reaction caused many problems in their lives, and I have now been able to step back and improve somewhat—though the overprotection is still there.*

Overall, Ann and I have a comfortable relationship and most of the insights she describes are things she came to herself as a result of talking with me rather than interpretations I made. She is much less anxious, stands up for herself, and her second marriage is far better than her first.

"Theodore" was a multitalented young man in his late twenties who I saw for eight years, three and four times a week, ending in 2003. He began therapy just after his wife had left him for another man. His father was emotionally distant and lacking in understanding and his mother a very disturbed and disturbing woman. Very bright, he quickly took to the therapy. In response to my question, he described several aspects of the therapy that were important, including our shared interests and his wish to be my favorite patient. We covered a number of issues related to his parents and late grandfather, who was one of the few supportive figures in his life. He concluded:

> To that effect, having the range to run my thoughts, explore the parameters, challenge my assumptions was probably the most important. I think what I achieved above all was a sense of refining my instrument of judgment, calibrating my self by revisiting those assumptions—senses, hunches, doubts, inklings—again and again, from every perspective, until I really could trust myself.

"Marie" was a woman I saw for seven years, once a week, ending in 2004. She was in her late thirties when we began, happily married, with two young children. She suffered from a great deal of anxiety that manifested itself in a variety of somatic symptoms, as well as inhibitions and low self-esteem. She was the middle of five children; her father had died when she was young and her older schizophrenic brother monopolized her mother's time and attention, leaving her neglected and having to care for herself.

> You are the best psychotherapist I ever had. I think altogether I've had five at various times during a twenty-five-year span. I'll try to explain what I think worked. One of the things that stands out is that your office seemed to be such a safe haven. No matter what turmoil I might be experiencing, everything was the same walking into your office. You were always the same, kind, attentive, supportive person waiting to hear what I had to say next. [I would add, that this was in contrast to her father who was involved with his sons and her mother who never had much time for her.] In addition, examining events and feelings over and over again changed me dramatically. Revisiting the same events and feelings over time seemed to do more than just take the sting away, they became innocuous.
>
> You helped me to see connections between events in my past and present along with the feelings associated with them. You told me that feelings are fact, a further validation that empowered me.
>
> From the beginning you made me feel that the time in your office was my time to use or not use. I was to lead the way with you there

*to help guide me to some insights, but the choice to accept or disre-
gard was always mine. Respect for me and my feelings was always
paramount.*

A number of factors are mentioned by Marie, including acceptance,
letting her set her own pace, support, and reliability. But insight also
seems central; she describes examining events over and over and
seeing connections between things in the past and present. And she
did change dramatically over the course of our work; her anxiety and
many related symptoms greatly diminished and she became much less
self-effacing and more assertive.

Concomitant Treatments

While I strongly believe that analytic therapy effects deep and lasting changes in people, I also do not think that other treatment methods,
engaged in at the same time, interfere with or "dilute" the analytic process. We therapists and patients need all the help we can get and, if medication works, or AA, or exercise, or meditation, I encourage my patients
to engage in these activities. Here I will present three examples that
illustrate the combining of psychotherapy with other approaches.

After ten years of very helpful analytic therapy, Alejandro felt it
wasn't working anymore and he began to explore other avenues.

Eventually I went on Wellbutrin [an antidepressant.] *The switch to
a psychiatrist was interesting, telling her what I was telling you, but
the therapy felt cold or out of date. The drug helped a lot, for a while.
I went off it and returned* [to therapy with me.] *In the last two years
I've seen a cognitive behaviorist. I can't compare the therapies fairly.
There's no depth to what I'm doing now, no dream interpretation, no
family history. There's only the present and the future. I don't know
what it would have been like, more than twenty-five years ago, if I
had walked into his office instead of yours. I doubt that I would have
achieved what I did...The first ten years of therapy...well...I've been
in one form of therapy or another since I was fifteen. So the first ten
years of therapy with you were thrilling, and I made large moral decisions, of a kind that I make now, knowing that some of these choices
are selfish and will cause pain to others. Later, I reached the limits
of something that only religion could begin to explore.* [Alejandro
became very involved in religion for a period, and, as was typical
of him, threw himself into it wholeheartedly.] *Religion gave me
an analytic framework that was much more useful than anything
close to the idea of spirituality, and in some ways the striving for a*

spiritual experience was a misunderstanding of the brilliance of that framework. But then even religion waned, when I saw it repeating its formulas, and I have seen culturally that the quest for religion doesn't have the fervor of the nineties.

My [cognitive behavioral] *therapy now seems to focus mostly on clarity of thought and action, not clarity of motive. Maybe that's too cute a formulation. It's a simpler system than psychoanalysis, more like coaching from someone with objectivity and wisdom that comes from a clarity about character.*

Alejandro's comments reflect his complexity as a thinker, his continuing search for both an ideal figure and a meaningful belief system, and his refusal to settle for dogma and easy answers. While he clearly states that he got a great deal out of our work together—I "saved his life" and "the first ten years of therapy...were thrilling"—he also said that after ten years, "something in the therapy wasn't working anymore."

Alejandro is a good example of someone who searches for growth in many places: psychoanalysis, antidepressant medication, religion, and cognitive-behavioral therapy. He took important things from each of these; all were helpful to him in their own ways.

A good deal of what he and I did in the therapy, especially in the early years, was cathartic—sometimes explosively so—as well as an exploration of his family background, the meaning of his dreams and fantasies, and the history and conflicts in his marriage and other relationships. I was somewhat in awe of his talent though from his comments one can see he was looking to me for wisdom and guidance. As time passed, we became much more comfortable with each other. Overall, my sense of what he got from his analysis was finding his ideal in himself. In my recent conversations with him, there is a confidence and lack of self-doubt, commensurate with his outstanding abilities, which he did not have at the beginning of his analysis.

Ruth was on antidepressant medication throughout the time I saw her and, in a recent conversation, told me she doesn't seem to need it anymore. Judith also found medication helpful:

But here's something else I should mention. Prozac did not exist when I was in analysis with you. I started to take P—prescribed by my regular doctor—about fourteen years ago. It changed my life and I am addicted. But I'm less neurotic, much more full of love and emotion in general, and I feel as if no matter how depressed I get...Prozac provides a pharmacological "safety net" that will prevent me from

91

falling into the abyss. I guess it's the next best thing to having a Dr. Breger to visit on a daily/weekly basis!

Oliver did some exploration of concomitant approaches while he was in analysis and many more after its completion:

I have received many sessions of other therapies since, mostly as very brief exposures to different techniques and modalities, both to benefit as the patient but probably more to learn as the perennial student/clinician. I received many hours of EMDR and of late, Somatic Experiencing. I studied and received many hours of hypnosis at one point. I'm studying bodywork more of late too so am exploring different modalities in that world too. I attribute the ease at which I access information internally to my time with you. It seemed few rocks were left unturned with you, so I had ready access to my internal world.

Money

An experienced colleague once said that if sex was the great taboo of the nineteenth century, money has taken its place now. There seems some truth to this; therapists are often reluctant to talk about their fees and patients sometimes feel freer to discuss their sexual exploits than their incomes. Freud early came up with the idea of "renting out" his time on a fixed basis and having patients pay for their sessions, whether they came or not, a practice no doubt related to the poverty of his early years. This was taken up and expanded by later psychoanalysts who routinely charged for missed sessions—whatever the patient's reason for not coming—and, in some cases, insisted that patients take their vacations at the same time as they did or be charged for the time. The rationale was that unless one made a financial sacrifice, the analysis would not be meaningful, a belief that was never subject to any test, and one that I think has no substance.

High and inflexible fees came to be the norm and these practices are not confined to classical psychoanalysts: I know at least some contemporary analytic therapists who pride themselves on charging the highest fees in the city. This seems to appeal to their sense that they are the best. Needless to say, such practices are very lucrative for the analyst, though often posing a hardship for the patient.

I will cite just one example. A woman analyst of an avowed contemporary orientation had been seeing a very depressed man for a number of years at her usual high fee. He went bankrupt and sank even deeper into despair and, due to this, didn't have the money to see her at the same fee. He was very attached to her after many years of therapy and was not keen to see someone else. She cut him back to once a month, which was all he could afford, and it did not occur to her to continue his treatment at a reduced fee, even though this was a particularly low point in his life. While she did not need the money, lowering her fee was just not something that a person of her stature did.

Several of my patients comment on my adjusting the fee to what they could afford. Judith, who had the first year of her analysis as a low-fee clinic case said:

> I adored the bond, the safety, the feeling of "privilege" at being able to have such a special relationship with you. Now, the fact that you got me into your program as a $10-a-session "experiment" may have added to that. Had I been expected to pay $75 a session—or whatever it was in those days—I may have felt differently...As my mother would have said, it wasn't just that I got psychoanalyzed. I got psychoanalyzed "wholesale." [My memory is that when the Clinic year was up we went through a stormy time, with her expressing a good deal of anger, around the raising of her fee.]

Christine speaks of my "generosity," Josh of my being "very giving to me...in terms of a reduced fee," and Yael, who will be discussed shortly: "You let me pay you way less than your usual fee for a long time." No doubt part of this came from my own working-class background—whatever they were paying seemed like a great deal of money compared to what I had as a child—but also, I like to think, from empathy, from sensing what it would mean to them. And from those instances where there is information, a reasonable fee, or even a very low one, was very therapeutic. Oliver describes how important my work with his fee was:

> In the financial department it seems to me you did something extraordinary with me. My mother died during the last year or so of the analysis. In the months awaiting the very small inheritance I received you went without receiving payment. Finally the inheritance came through and I paid off your bill to the tune of something like $5000. I handed you the check and you said thank you, nothing more. Even now that is not a small sum. So your patience and your lack of financial stress permitted a faith in me, mirrored that I could be trusted to be good to my word. That helped me enormously...and had a great impact on me, primarily in the role-model department. In my clinical work my handling of money with patients has very rarely ever been a problem.

Silence and Talking

The forever-silent analyst has become a cliché. In Woody Allen's *Annie Hall*, Diane Keaton is telling him about things her analyst said and Allen says, with amazement, "He talks to you?" Modern analytic therapy is not bound by the old rules of abstinence, anonymity, and neutrality, of course, but whether silence or talking will be therapeutic must be decided for each individual patient and at each particular time in the treatment. A writer friend described her analyst's silence as most helpful since she had been immersed all her life in "words" and this was a time where she experienced his not speaking as a safe, accepting environment in which she could, "possess my own judgments."

There were a variety of reactions to my talking or not talking. Judith found lying on the couch essential and saw it as important that I let her "blather on," while Scott "never totally bought into the Freudian thing." Isaac felt that he didn't want me to talk until well into the analysis since he needed a comfortable place to "let out my steam." Socrates, on the other hand, found the relative silence in our early sessions very uncomfortable but it eventually led to his letting loose a torrent of emotions that was a real turning point. Alejandro required me to be silent in the beginning, "like a real psychoanalyst," while Leo, in contrast, having come from years with a silent analyst, needed an open give and take from the outset. Andrew, who also began his treatment with me after extremely disappointing contacts with two other analysts, noted how vital my "humane" comments were from the very beginning of our work.

I have also found that mentioning details about a patient's life, or things they have brought up in previous sessions, shows that I have really been listening closely; that they are important enough for me to remember them. This is a particular kind of talking; it demonstrates that they exist in my mind in the time between sessions.

Two Special Cases

A number of the patients I have discussed so far have been therapists themselves, creative writers, and individuals who have had some prior therapy or analysis. "Nate" is in a different category. I began seeing him when he was fourteen years old and had just begun attending a high-powered private school, where he immediately felt overwhelmed. Because of his age, I also had sessions with his mother, father, and all three of them together. From my extensive contact with the family, I became convinced that his social difficulties and extreme anxiety were inborn predispositions. It took me a while to become convinced of this—for a time I looked for causes of his troubles in the ways his mother and father treated him—but a careful examination of the family, as well as other factors, supported the view of genetically based anxiety.

In the heyday of psychoanalysis, of course, when interpretations were recklessly thrown about, his symptoms, like those of autistic children, would have been blamed on faulty parenting. Countering this idea, I observed how, despite the fact that he caused considerable worry for his parents for a number of years, they have remained supportive and committed to his welfare. Nate and I began meeting once a week, and sometimes twice, and I was impressed with his ability and desire to use me and the therapy despite his youth and lack of prior experience. He is now thirty and we continue to have telephone contact about once a month.

Because of the unusual level of his anxiety I had him undergo neuropsychological testing, which confirmed the biological basis of his difficulties and several psychiatric drugs were tried with some small effect. His major mode of coping, from late childhood on, was to stay in his room and withdraw into the world of comic book heroes, most specifically, Superman, with whom he strongly identified. He was not so out of touch with reality that he thought he was Superman, but he hoped that somehow he would be revealed as his hero though some vague act of divine justice. Despite his withdrawn state, he managed to finish high school at a smaller, less pressured institution, and to graduate, with some difficulty, from a liberal arts college. But his degree did not point to any specific career and he drifted for a time between low-level jobs. During his final years of college he carried on a love affair with an older woman he met through an adult phone service. His description of the affair, as well as her letters which he showed me, indicated her affection and genuine interest in him. But aside from her, he had no friends, male or female, outside his family. At present, he has completed postgraduate training and is working successfully at a professional job.

I should mention that, despite pleas from his parents that I see him more than once a week, I came to understand that it was vital to his sense of developing independence that he call me when he felt the need for an appointment. Here is his own account:

> *I can't identify a single period in therapy that was the most helpful. We have been working together since I was fourteen years old; and*

I was very different back then! Lost in fantasy, obsessed with female sexuality, devastated by cutthroat classmates, fighting with my parents, and worried about my "small head."[2] It was not a good time. I could very well have wound up in a mental hospital if not for the dependability of our therapy sessions. The number of mental and emotional steps taken is countless. It has been a slow and gradual process of calming my mind and forging an identity.

The first several years were a brute confrontation with amorphous adolescent anxiety. This led to a modicum of self-awareness and further confrontation with the existential problems of living and the pointless trajectory of my life. And all roads led to the root problem of my innately fearful nature.

A constant theme has been me describing a nightmare vision of how I see myself and the world. In this nightmare, I fail to accomplish anything of value and everything that I hate succeeds. Therapy helps prevent this idea from overwhelming me and spiraling out of control. It puts things into a perspective where I can see the good in life, believe in the good...or simply force my mind not to think about all that bullshit so I can endure.

Tony Soprano says therapy is like "taking a shit." This is absolutely true. It's just an enormous pressure release. A feeling of being understood; of not being alone. In the "real world" my identity can fluctuate from moment to moment or person to person. In therapy I always know who I am and what I really believe. It's a bedrock.

The most concrete progress has occurred in the last few years as I've made headway in working and living as a functional adult. A lot of my therapy has had to do with letting all the childhood hopes just wither away. Realizing how all the grandiose options and potential I squandered never really existed. It was actually a relief. To honestly see the good qualities I possess is a relief. Knowing what's real is a relief. Growing up is a relief. Because if you don't grow up, you just twist in the wind your whole life, even if you don't know it. But I knew I was twisting in the wind. And I knew I needed help.

Almost a year after writing the above, Nate had taken the final step into adulthood, beginning to date and finding a girlfriend. We had a session in which he showed that he had arrived at a whole new, more mature, way of thinking about himself. As he put it:

Therapy is a powerful guide, but I've reached a saturation point. A point where I just can't stand parsing everything to death. Agonizing over the moral and emotional relevance of every little thing must come to an end. What good is self-awareness if it just becomes another facet of the paralysis? Another facet of escapism? It's time to control my reactions. It's time to transcend the need to categorize everything as good or bad and right and wrong. It's a cliche, but I have to internalize the old Serenity Prayer: "God, grant me the serenity to accept the things I cannot change, courage to change the things I can, And wisdom to know the difference." I am satisfied that I fully understand myself and my issues. I am satisfied that Dr. Breger fully understands what I've told him and that he is my friend who I can always talk to.

As I review my role in Nate's therapy, I think what was particularly helpful from my side was that I always believed in him, always felt he could overcome the nearly overwhelming fears he struggled with, never consigned him, even in my private thoughts, to a hopeless diagnosis, though he certainly seemed pretty close to the edge at times. This was no doubt communicated to him in a variety of ways. The main thing I talked about was how extremely anxious he was and how his efforts to deal with this created additional problems, for example, by drifting into fantasy states or endlessly obsessing about his problems, focusing on every possible meaning, instead of studying for an exam. The rest of the time I was primarily a listener as he expressed his terror, described his dreams and fantasies, cried, spun out his ideas about other people, the world, and his place in it. As he told me on more than one occasion, I am the one person who knows all about him, so that talking to me helps him to feel organized, calm, and not alone. More recently, he has come to feel his Dad is also someone who truly understands him and who he can confide in—perhaps as a result of all our work together—though this was not true earlier.

"Yael" was just a year or two out of college when she first came to see me many years ago. We met five times a week, initially face to face, and then with her lying on the couch and then, again, sitting up. The frequency of sessions tapered down over the years and we now speak every other week on the telephone. When she began her therapy she was still reeling from the death of her mother that occurred during her sophomore year in college. She was extremely anxious, suffered enormous guilt focused on her mother's death—she was not "allowed" to have a real life of her own—had many fears about her health and body, and tried to manage all of this with a variety of obsessions and compulsions. Her account covers almost all the features of analytic psychotherapy.

Here are some thoughts about what I have found to be most healing about my work with you. Let me first say that all of it's been healing. Absolutely all. There is nothing I would change.

Compassion: I could see it in your eyes from the moment I met you in your office. Maybe that's why I had my troubles with eye contact [for a long time she could not look directly at me and no attempts to understand this seemed to have any effect.] *It was too good to be true. I sensed that you were bigger than my despair and could handle it. I felt that I was in excellent hands.*

Attunement: I have always felt that you got me, that you could really understand why my particular life experience was difficult for me. That was a completely new experience for me, having grown up in a family full of denial and secrets and illusions to uphold.

Listening: You listen carefully and intently. You respond to what I need to share and where I need to go and don't make assumptions or lead me in another direction.

Insight: Over the years you will say things that unlock some old mystery and set me free.

Intensity: I sensed your intensity from the start, too. And it reassured me. I had sometimes gotten the message that I was too intense, but I wasn't too intense for you.

Equanimity: I could tell you what I thought were the most awful things about me and about my life and you never seemed to miss a beat. You reassure me that I'm not a bad person and that I deserve to have a life. And it is extremely helpful when you just come out and say that, which I know that some analysts/therapists would never do in a million years.

Non-Defensiveness: I've been able to tell you the few times I have been angry with you and you have never gotten reactive. It felt very, very respectful. You let me really process my transference issues over your divorce and it was enormously helpful to me [She had had a strong reaction to her own parents' divorce when she was eight, which was re-aroused by my divorce in 1987.]

Time: You've given me all the time in the world. As you've heard many many times I used to follow Mom around and try to get her to spend time with me and hear my stories and I could never get her to stop and listen and attend. I have really needed it and benefited from it.

Self-Disclosure/Intuition: In the beginning of my work with you I couldn't handle knowing much about your life and you completely honored that. Over time I wanted to know more and you honored that.

Everything you've ever shared about your personal life has meant a tremendous amount to me and has deepened my work with you.

Normalizing: You let me know that I'm not alone, that other people think and feel and go through some of the same things, too, things that I have tormented myself about needlessly. You've helped me to discover what it means to be a human being.

Conscientiousness: You have been reliable to a fault. Even when you've had very serious medical issues to deal with you have been quicker to get back to work than seems humanly possible. [The old workaholism has its beneficial side, at least for patients.]

Friendship: As the years have gone on the friendship aspect of my relationship with you has grown and has made me feel like a more worthy person. It meant so much to me that you were at our wedding. I wanted you and your wife to come to my son's Bar Mitzvah and was so sorry that your medical situation at the time prevented it. These days I've appreciated it when you congratulate my husband on his...projects.

Music: You may not see this as therapy but it has meant so much to me when you have shared your music. [I sent her a couple of CDs when she mentioned being a fan of a musician I also liked.] *I treasure everything you've sent. And it is truly therapeutic for me when I listen to it.*

Support: You reassured me that I should go ahead and have a child. You got me through those very difficult last three months of my pregnancy. You were very happy for us when my son was born and very sweet to him when we bumped into you at the bookstore; he was about three and I told him that you were the guy who "helps me with my feelings."

Forgiveness: Because of you I have forgiven myself and come to accept myself in ways that I never could have predicted. In the early days I was such a crazy mixed-up kid, so distraught and fearful and full of guilt. I am not absolutely all the way there, but I am moving in the direction of letting myself be.

I began Yael's treatment when I was starting my own psychoanalytic training and more under Freud's influence than I later became; she and I changed and evolved together. One of her prominent obsessive fears was that her reproductive organs would be damaged, preventing her from having children. This was part of a larger system of ideas related to her mother's death, which occurred just when she was leaving home to begin her own independent life. In her mind, she was to be punished by not being allowed to have her own life, and certainly not to become a mother, because of her overwhelming guilt. We worked and reworked this complicated set of beliefs, seeking to disconfirm them, and, eventually, she permitted herself to get pregnant. By chance—or fate—the birth of her child was accompanied by a number of medical complications, although she and the baby survived. She and her husband have successfully raised this son, not without a fair amount of anxiety that she was able to contain thanks, I like to believe, to all our therapeutic work, and he has turned out to be a talented and happy young man, about to finish college.

Transference

I should say a word about transference since, in my view, it is one of Freud's most original discoveries. All patients display transference; that is, the way they relate to the therapist reflects the enduring, typically unconscious, patterns of their emotional relationships. Observing the patient's transference reactions is a valuable way to understand them. On the other hand, I have come to think that transference interpretations—pointing out such reactions to the patient—are not necessarily helpful, indeed, can sometimes be experienced as criticism. This is still another way in which contemporary analytic therapy differs from classical psychoanalysis, which values transference interpretations over all other interventions.[3]

What Is Effective in Analytic Psychotherapy

The therapeutic outcomes in almost all the cases reviewed here included marked reductions in anxiety, the lifting of depression, increases in self-esteem and self-acceptance, the abatement—if not complete removal—of a variety of symptoms, and changing old relationship patterns. And, it is clear that the relationship between the patients and myself was at the heart of these successful outcomes, though it took different forms with each individual. Experiencing my attention and affection, admitting and repairing mistakes, catharsis, insight gained from collaboratively constructed interpretations, self-disclosure, humor, flexible fees, and openness to concomitant forms of treatment, all played their roles. In all the cases discussed so far, one can see that how close or distant you are with each patient, when to openly express liking, respect or admiration and when not, are complicated questions. How much to disclose about yourself and when to do it must, again, be puzzled out for each individual. Similarly, with the question of when to talk and when to be silent, when to use humor, or share common interests, and how to handle the inevitable mistakes that occur in the course of treatment. Then there are questions of the way in which interpretations are made—they should be individually crafted for each patient—and insights conveyed, and when to recommend concomitant treatments. If you handle all these issues reasonably well, are empathic and stay tuned to the patient's needs and emotions, admit your mistakes and work at repairing them, these patient reports show how analytic psychotherapy produces enduring changes that are profoundly transformative.

9

When I Didn't Help

While I still do believe there's value in learning to question your family's view of things, I also feel that talk therapy ends with a big, "Yeah, so?"—at least for me.

—Deborah

With each major failure on your part, I began to lose confidence that you knew what you were doing.

—Karl

The patients described in the preceding chapters had life-changing experiences in their therapies. As noted earlier, they constitute a skewed sample since those whose therapy was not helpful were less likely to respond to my questionnaire. There were also a small number of former patients whom I did not contact since I only saw them briefly or knew they were unhappy with the results and would not have been pleased to hear from me. Here, I wish to discuss patients for whom my kind of analysis was only minimally helpful, if it worked at all, as well as others where special problems arose. I hope this will dispel any idea that the kind of analysis I practice is still another "pure gold" that can help everyone. There is also the factor of therapist–patient match; like everyone else, I work well with some people and not so well with others.

The first group of patients where things did not turn out well consists of those who never made a connection with me. Every therapist has his own way of working when first meeting a patient. I typically begin by saying that I am a contemporary, analytically oriented therapist, and that they will find out what this means from what goes on between us. This may be taken to mean that I am eclectic or a wishy-washy flip-flopper, not what some patients, at least at the beginning, want if they are looking for a strong doctor-therapist who knows what he is doing.

Some therapists begin by doing an extensive diagnostic interview and collect a detailed life history with the aim of arriving at a formulation of character structure and dynamics. As should be clear by now, patients are complex, unique individuals who cannot be reduced to a diagnostic label such as those found in the DSM (Diagnostic and Statistical Manual). This is one reason why outcome studies for "evidenced based" treatments—which, as a common example, presumably demonstrate the effectiveness of some form of short treatment with "anxiety disorders" or "depression"—are based on false assumptions. The things my patients work on cannot be captured in a diagnostic label; they involve the whole person and his or her history and relationships, and these take a good deal of time to understand and change. For an extensive discussion of this issue, covering scientific, historical and cultural factors, see Wampold (2001), whose conclusions support the position taken here. Marcia Angell (2011a) also provides a thoroughgoing critique of the psychiatric diagnostic enterprise.

The assumption of using the categories in the DSM is that gathering this information will allow one to make a decision about whether the person is treatable and, if so, how best to proceed. While I certainly pay attention to whatever is reported in the initial interview—for example, I would want to know if the person is someone that I could not work with, where the fit between us feels wrong—I don't like structuring the first meeting in this way; it puts me too much in the position of an authority with the patient as passive recipient of my expertise. It is like someone reporting their symptoms to a medical doctor who will diagnose their disease and order the required treatment. Rather than diagnose and prescribe, I prefer to give the potential patient, from the first session, a chance to see what working with me in a collaborative way will be like. Some analysts tell new patients that they will see them for a "trial period" of three or four sessions before deciding whether or not to accept them for treatment. I don't think this is a good idea; it hardly promotes spontaneity since the patient is literally on trial to see if he or she is good enough to be seen.

I typically open the first session by asking, "What brings you here" or "Where would you like to begin?" and we are off and running. I mainly listen at first and, if they are uncomfortable with my not saying much, tell them that I have to get to know them better before I can say anything, but I will not be a silent psychoanalyst. If I can think of some response that conveys my empathy or understanding, I don't hesitate to make it, though often it takes a session or two before

I know enough to say anything meaningful. And far from looking for "analyzable" patients, I have always been open to seeing anyone, with a few exceptions, who is willing to give it a try.

Some patients like my approach and some don't and within a few sessions—sometimes even after a single session—they see what kind of therapist I am and can make their own decision about whether to continue. I recall one young man who, in response to my opening remark, "Where would you like to start?" went into a tirade about how I was one of those psychoanalysts who put the whole burden on him, how I would never talk or tell him anything, and on and on. Needless to say, he never came back. More common are those who come a few times and then stop, typically without telling me why—and often without paying their bill. From what they reveal I can discern anxiety, unhappiness, serious problems in their relationships, and other troubles that could be helped by therapy, but this group, for a variety of reasons, is not willing to engage, at least not with me. While one can put the blame on them—they are too resistant, too threatened by self-exposure, or just not comfortable talking about themselves—I prefer to think that they got a sample of who I am and my type of therapy and decided it wasn't what they wanted.

A second group is made up of those who come to see me for some time but never make a very deep or strong connection. There are a variety of people in this group; some get a certain amount of help but, overall, are dissatisfied. Others get something out of the therapy though from my perspective there appears to be much more that could be accomplished.

"Deborah" and her husband, both highly educated, creative individuals, had a first child who was autistic. This put a great strain on the marriage and they began couple's therapy with a colleague who eventually saw the husband individually and referred Deborah to me. We met once a week for three and a half years, ending in 1999.

> *I do think one way in which therapy helps in general is simply that it takes someone out of the narrow confines of the opinions he/she's grown up with. I do, for example, remember that one time I defended my father's lack of nurturing by saying "well, men of that generation were like that" and you pointed out that you were basically a "man of that generation" and you spent a lot of time taking care of your children. It was a nice moment of clarity and helped me step outside of the viewpoint I'd grown up never questioning. And of course those*

moments generalize into an overall realization that so much of what we take to be "truth" is simply the point of view our parents imposed on us—maybe unconsciously—at such an early age that it FEELS objective and absolute when it's neither.

That said, I have to admit that I'm a recent convert to the idea of cognitive-behavioral therapy as opposed to the more traditional "talking" kind. My daughter appears to be on the OCD [obsessive compulsive disorder] spectrum. For a while she was seeing a Cognitive Behavioral therapist and I was sitting in on those sessions and was impressed enough to get a book about CBT for myself—"When Panic Attacks"— since I still have huge anxiety issues. The idea of working on changing behaviors first and allowing everything else to follow makes good sense to me. Of course, I come already primed in favor of a behavioral approach because that's what we used with my son who has autism and it worked wonders. While I still do believe there's value in learning to question your family's view of things, I also feel that talk therapy ends with a big, "Yeah, so?"—at least for me. Okay, so my father was fairly critical: I can sit around and keep thinking and complaining about it, or I can simply work on my own tendencies to be self-critical by recognizing them and coming up with an exercise that successfully combats them. In other words, I'm not sure that it matters so much WHY we are the way we are; I feel like what matters is that we find a way to become happier and healthier in spite of all that. And the very act of taking control and changing something is incredibly empowering and encouraging in itself. Whereas—not to rag on talk therapy, sorry—relying on someone else to listen to you and ask questions feels like it's creating an unhealthy dependence.

I felt that the kind of psychotherapy I practice was basically not for her; that it was, at best, minimally helpful. While she retained some insights connecting her father's criticisms to her own tendency toward self-criticism, she still has "huge anxiety issues" and is finding cognitive behavioral therapy more helpful. At the same time, in response to her reading the above, she said:

I should point out that in a way the therapy WAS successful. My husband and I originally sought therapy for marital problems and we're celebrating our twenty-first anniversary next week. I can't think of anyone who has a stronger marriage than ours, although I do wish he'd stop leaving that light on in the closet.

"Karl" was an experienced therapist I saw once a week for four years, ending in 2003, and for another two years, ending in 2006.

He had been in treatment with a great number of psychoanalysts and psychotherapists over many years and, while a few may have helped him, his overall view was that these treatments were worthless. Well into our work, he was hospitalized after a postsurgical accident, and my wife and I visited him twice in the hospital, which he felt was one of the few helpful things that occurred during the therapy.[1] Here is his account:

> *I don't want to go into telling you what you did right and what you did wrong. You were patient, didn't reject me and sort of reacted sort of OK to my direct and blunt criticisms but all in all I don't think you knew who I was or who I am and could not put yourself in my shoes in life. Few can. You will just have to struggle with that…working from so-called attachment theory was all you continued to want to do to draw me closer to you for your needs. You and your wife—she was part of my therapy too, in case you have forgotten—were very good, especially in and out of the hospital. But I don't want to rehash all this. With each major failure on your part, I began to lose confidence that you knew what you were doing…*

> *PS: Anything to do with "attachment theory" and pulling for me to be dependent was all, all wrong for what I am doing in life. All the things I like about myself and am proud of in myself you were bothered by or regarded as defending myself. Not true. You almost, but not quite, came across as sarcastic.*

> *If the person achieves their goals, the therapy is helpful. If the patient doesn't achieve their goals or rarely changes much, then the therapy is unhelpful. Go figure…I can only say that in my 40+ years of seeking out someone who would get me, none—except you and T—have done that. And of course the psychoanalytic mode usually places the responsibility on the patient but in fact most therapists are quite incompetent and are not very smart or empathic. How can all of them be that way? Easy. They are. Or else they are too middle class and have not had especially traumatic lives and their psychology is so far removed from the patient's that all they can do is be "empathic" but never act like active, sound, surrogate parents. They fear acting with authority…They are passive rather than active. They really don't feel they are responsible for how the patient turns out and how the therapy goes.*

Karl's overall sense is that, while "T" and I—another therapist he saw at the same time—"got him" some of the time, by and large, I failed him. Since some of the therapists he saw at an earlier period were classical Freudians, I began our therapy thinking that he was right in his negative appraisals of them, and that I could do better. And we did seem to make some progress at first. But, as time passed, it became clear that I was, overall, another in the long line of therapists who had not really helped him. He is right that, for a time, I focused on the anxiety he experienced if he became too close and experienced emotions—his references to my "attachment theory" approach—but, even after I backed off from that, or maybe because I had stressed it for a while, I was ultimately seen as another of the many therapists who were unable to provide him with the help he sought. Among other things, this may demonstrate that my stress on attachment, while helpful with many patients, was not right for him. As he said, "Go figure!"

I turn now to some patients for whom personal qualities of mine interfered with the potential success of treatment: "countertransference" problems in the traditional lingo. The first comes from the control—or over-control—of my emotions. Several patients who had very helpful experiences commented on my steadiness, unflappability, the way they could always count on me to be there, no matter how much fear, anger, sadness, or other intense feelings they might express. While, in those cases, my control was a useful part of the treatment, there were others in which it led to an insensitivity to the patient's pain that interfered with a successful outcome. I think of two cases, seen a number of years ago, where this was so.

The first was a woman in her late twenties whom I will call "Amy"; she came to see me suffering with intense anxiety. While in her professional life she was a very competent and in-charge young woman, in sessions she became so agitated that she would unthinkingly twist the buttons off her coat and the clasps off her purse. She had never been in therapy, nor talked with anyone about herself—speaking with outsiders about family matters was strictly forbidden by her parents—but her childhood, which she gradually revealed, was a combination of harshness and trauma. She was one of several children and grew up in a milieu where they all were expected to perform as tennis players at the highest possible level. She rebelled a little against this demanding regime by choosing to become a gymnast, though endless hours of practice were still required. When she was thirteen she was sexually molested by a man her parents knew, and when she tried to tell her father about this, his response was, "He would never do that." This shut off any further communication about the molestation until she revealed it, with much shame and fear, years later in her therapy with me. In her adolescence, she dealt with the family's demands, and her trauma, by stealing alcohol from her parent's liquor cabinet and dulling her emotional turmoil with it. They never seemed aware that their gin was diluted with water, nor that anything was troubling their daughter.

As Amy revealed this history to me it seemed clear that she had a great deal to work on in therapy. And while I did not push her in an obvious way, she must have picked up signs that the sexual molestation and insensitive treatment by her parents were things I thought it important to talk about. It was too much for her and she stopped coming. Looking back—or if I could see her in later years when I knew more—I think I would have tried to slow her down, counseled her to only talk about these frightening and shameful matters gradually, lest she be overwhelmed. But, being someone who typically damped down my own emotions, I was not attuned to how difficult it was for her, and she stopped the therapy before we could make much progress.

The second case is a man I will call "Thomas," who came for therapy in his late thirties. He had talent in a number of artistic fields but could not settle down for long in any one of them. In addition, while he had a few male acquaintances, and seemed a pleasant and attractive man, he had never had a lasting relationship with a woman. Therapy proceeded with him gradually revealing more and more about himself and his childhood. And as I became acquainted with his background, it appeared, like Amy's, to be a horror that was never spoken about: a combination of distance, harshness, and emotional insensitivity which, given his artistic nature, was an even more significant deprivation than it might have been for someone else. I recall one incident from when he was young in which his policeman father had Thomas' beloved dog killed because it was barking too much and, when the frightened small boy went to his mother and asked, "Will we all die?" she responded in a matter of fact manner: "Yes."

As the therapy proceeded—Thomas saw me once a week for over a year in the 1970s—it became clear that there was a great deal of fear and pain behind his bland and friendly façade. I recall one dream in particular in which he had an infected arm which, when cut, let loose a stream of pus that poured out without end. In retrospect, I see this as a symbol for all the terrible emotion and pain that was being unleashed in his therapy but, as in the case of Amy, I was not sufficiently aware of the strength of his terror, and he stopped therapy shortly after reporting this dream. I made a couple of attempts to contact him to discuss his leaving but he wasn't willing to come back.

Amy and Thomas illustrate difficulties related to my emotional control. It is not that I didn't want my patients to express everything they felt; I encouraged them to do so. But it was comfortable for me to go through all these emotions vicariously, from my safe position as therapist. They were the ones directly feeling these things, after all, not I. While catharsis was very helpful to a number of patients, I think my own conflicts about the expression of emotion led to insensitivity in these two cases.

Another kind of problem stems from my exaggerated sense of responsibility and tendency toward excessive guilt which, again, was helpful with many of the patients, who commented on my trustworthiness, reliability, and related qualities. But there have been a few patients who picked up on my propensity to feel guilty and used it to manipulate me in ways that were not therapeutic for them, nor comfortable for me. While in general I don't like to use diagnostic labels, there is a specific group of patients who are hard to discuss without resorting to this. I refer to those called "borderlines" or "borderline personality disorders."[2] They are individuals with very labile emotions, typically very anxious, given to black and white perceptions of people and the world, frequently hostile, and prone to blame others for the things that go wrong in their lives. Some report very traumatic histories, while others claim to have such backgrounds even if it is not clear that they had. They are, needless to say, very difficult to treat and many have a history of moving from one therapist to another, shopping for medication and/or someone who will confirm their belief that they are mistreated by the world. Not uncommonly, borderline patients will pressure their therapists with suicide threats, self-mutilation, and the like, demanding concessions of various kinds. Only if they are given these things will they feel really loved and accepted, only then will their fears be calmed. If the therapist gives in to such pressure the stakes are raised; bending the rules produces temporary relief and the struggle over limitations starts up again.

Few therapists I know find borderline patients easy to work with, and I have had my own particular problems with them. There is a history of suicide in my family of origin and, while I am aware of my special sensitivity to suicide threats, and try to use this understanding so that my feelings don't interfere with patients' freedom to express their thoughts and fantasies about killing themselves, certain patients have no doubt picked up on my sensitivity in this area and used it in attempts to control me. I have come to see that these patients require the setting of limits and boundaries if they are to get any help from therapy, and that they frequently quit if you attempt to set such boundaries, but can sometimes be helped if they can work within a firm, well-structured relationship.

Another kind of problem, related to my tendency toward feeling guilty, is what I now jokingly call my "pathological modesty." While in many ways I have been quite competitive and driven toward accomplishments and success, a lot of this is what Alfred Adler would call an over-compensation for a sense of inferiority. To many of my patients, my informal manner and the fact that I did not flaunt my position or accomplishments made my office a safe haven, a place where they knew their needs came first, where they could set the pace, and that I was someone they could trust and be open with. But especially early in my career the "modesty" was over-done. Since my hero as a boy was The Lone Ranger, someone who does not have a self, or even a name—"Who was that masked man anyway?"—and other movie cowboys, when patients would compliment me or talk about a book I had published, I would do a version of "Aw shucks, it warn't nothin.'" This interfered with their desire to see me as an idealized figure, an important childhood need, as Kohut has shown. The case of Rory, described earlier, is a clear illustration of how having me as an analyst who was both accepting and accomplished was very important to him. Ruth commented that she chose me because of my stature in ICP: "You were the senior guy, like my Dad was in his firm. That felt safe and familiar to me, I felt I would be protected." If I had gone into my modesty routine with these patients, it would have interfered with their need to see me as a strong, accomplished, and idealized figure. In sum, like every therapist, I have my own particular shortcomings, which have been helpful with some patients and caused unnecessary problems with others.

10

Endings

*Termination was handled without clinging on your part, Whew! Lastly, at the very end, I sat up and asked you every personal question that mattered to me. **You answered them all.** That was amazing and healing.*

—Oliver

The kind of analytic therapy that I practice can pose special problems when the patient and I feel we have completed our work. Many of the patients described in the preceding chapters were seen for a number of years, made significant improvements in their lives, learned a great deal about themselves, and developed a powerful connection with me, a bond that went both ways. I have found that it is impossible to work at a deep emotional level with people over long periods without developing real affection for them. Such feelings are absolutely necessary for effective treatment, but when the therapy is over, what will become of this treasured relationship? Shall we become friends and socialize? If we do, what role will our spouses play? Can one maintain a real friendship, or would one want to, with every former patient? Would all patients want to have me in their lives as a friend? Transference aspects of the relationship don't simply vanish when the therapy is officially over. And then there is another difficult problem in posttherapy contact: if the therapist continues a social relationship or friendship with a former patient, is he doing it because it is good for the patient or because he must keep them in his orbit for his own needs?

Classical psychoanalysis solves the problem by forbidding posttherapy contact, by defining it as antipsychoanalytic, just as friendly, open, or self-disclosing interactions during analysis are taboo. Since I, and other contemporary analysts, don't agree with these old strictures, we are much more open and friendly during the treatment, but are then faced with a different kind of problem when the therapy is completed. Once again, the new fundamental rule can serve as a guide: therapy—or in this case, posttherapy contact—must be for the patient's needs and not the analyst's, though one must discover how to apply this guideline in each particular case.

Here is Oliver's account of the end of our work together:

> *Termination was handled without clinging on your part. Whew! You encouraged a few more months after I announced my feeling done and the timing was perfect. That helped me. You accepted a gift of a psychic reading from my teacher at that time. It seemed extraordinary that what I perceived as "stodgy old you" would be curious enough to go. You did go, and although you were skeptical and slightly cynical even after you went, you went. That was rewarding to me. Lastly, at the very end, I sat up and asked you every personal question that mattered to me. **You answered them all.** That was amazing and healing.*

I saw Scott for ten years and, as his own account reveals, the analysis helped him turn his life around and, in the later phases, he felt I was "a friend and supporter." When we ended the analysis by mutual agreement, we met for lunch a few months later, and he seemed comfortable asking me more about my own life. My wife and I invited him and Pati over to dinner one time. We now keep in touch with a yearly holiday card, in which he brings me up-to-date on such things as his new grandchild, his continuing happy marriage, and developments in his career. He doesn't want or require any more contact than this.

Christine and I had some brief contacts outside the office in the later years of her analysis and, when it was finished, she invited my wife and me to her house for dinner as a gesture of appreciation. There, we met her husband and two dogs, saw photos of the mother we had spent so much time talking about, and got a sense of the way they lived. As it turned out, my wife has always been a great dog lover and, when we acquired two Labradors, we arranged to meet Christine and her husband at a dog park where all of us—humans plus dogs—could interact. Since then, they have moved far away and we maintain friendly contact by e-mail. She has developed a close relationship with my wife; as she put it:

> *I think that, at the beginning, part of my communicating with Barbara, rather than you—apart from the fact that I felt a connection with her—was that it was easier, a residue of I might be bothering/boring you. I did always think that you were incredibly busy, but that I had your attention in sessions. Barbara has always been so openly welcoming, encouraging and friendly, not that you have not been all*

of those things too. Then I feel that, over time, a really deep and warm relationship developed between her and me, which I am very happy about. But of course you are always there and I know that whatever I communicate to her, gets passed on to you.

MaryAnn has also moved to another city and never fails to send me a small gift on my birthday, addressed to "Papa Luigi," and letting me know about her living situation and the work she is doing. As a therapist, she is amazing, donating a large amount of her time to working with traumatized war veterans free of charge. She, too, is a great animal lover, so she and my wife have some correspondence about that.

Leo and Alejandro, the two writers that I saw for many years, don't feel much need to stay in touch though I like to hear from them occasionally just to know what is happening with their lives, writing projects, and children, who were all born during the years of their analyses and feel somewhat like grandchildren to me. Leo and I have met for lunch a few times over the last years and when I contacted him to get his answer to the questionnaire, we had a spirited phone conversation in which he expressed his enthusiasm for my project and brought me up-to-date on his life. With both men, it is clear that we feel real affection for each other, but also clear that they are very busy and don't particularly need more contact with me.

Josh gave a very generous going away party for my wife and me when we were leaving Los Angeles, and he and I now stay in touch with an occasional note or phone call. When he, his wife, and two boys were on a vacation in Northern California, we all got together for dinner. It was great to see his sons who, again, I feel I have known since they were born, and it was very pleasant to spend time with the whole family. Both Ruth and Isabella are therapists; we have encountered each other several times at professional meetings and conferences and Ruth and I met for breakfast a few years after the end of her analysis. As with many of the others, we are always glad to see each other, there are obvious good feelings, but they do not feel the need for more social contact. This is true of a number of my other former patients: Socrates, Isaac, Seth, and still others who are not included in this book. Our contact posttherapy is confined to a once-a-year holiday card—if that—usually with a note catching me up on events in their lives, to which I respond with a similar message.

Andrew married a lovely woman toward the end of his analysis and they moved to a distant city; we stay in contact by e-mail. Though

I wasn't aware of it when I was seeing him, it turns out we—in fact all four of us—have shared interests in music, novels, writing projects, movies, and enjoy swapping CDs and books. On a couple of occasions they have visited our area, and we have spent enjoyable social time together, something that I believe will continue. This same pattern characterizes my postanalysis contact with Theodore; he and his wife moved out of Los Angeles and had a son whose growth I am informed of by e-mail photographs. They dropped in for a visit once when they were in the area and we will probably see them again since, as is true of Andrew and his wife, we have a number of interests in common.

The reader may be wondering if these continuing posttherapy contacts didn't deprive my patients of working through issues that arise with a fixed ending. Classical psychoanalysis describes the ideal treatment as going through three phases: "initial," "middle," and "termination." During the middle phase the deepest work is done, the patient "regresses" and gets in touch with unconscious material from the earliest years. As this is worked through, a termination date is fixed, typically six months to a year in advance, and this sets off a resurgence of unconscious material, as well as bringing up specific issues related to loss, which can then be worked through. Or so the theory has it. With a few of my patients, something like this seemed to occur; setting a specific ending date to the treatment did, indeed, allow us to do further exploration of their experiences of loss, rejection, or death of loved ones. Judith, whose analysis fits the classical pattern more than any of my other patients, described the termination as, "Only that I felt ready, proud to have gotten there, yet sad to leave you. Like a kid going off to college!" I have not observed any standard reaction with all patients; one psychoanalytic pattern does not fit everyone. I leave the ending of treatment up to the patient and make clear that, should difficult life issues or crises arise, they are free to contact me.

As I look over the posttherapy relationships with all these former patients, they feel fairly comfortable. As much as possible I have followed their lead, having as much or as little contact as they want. My wife and I have attended a few weddings and bar mitzvahs and I know it has been very important to the patients who invited us that we were there. For others, it would have made them uncomfortable to have me attend such events.

While analysis can bring up child-like feelings, its goal should be to work these through to mature independence. The way contemporary analysis is practiced—with the emphasis on an open, friendly relationship—may be used as a rationale for keeping ex-patients in one's life, even when it is not best for them. Maintaining a friendly or social relationship posttherapy doesn't preclude the patient's independence, but one must always guard against using former patients for one's own needs.

My Practice Comes to an End

I turn now to the way my practice in Los Angeles came to its conclusion. Several of the patients in the previous chapters made reference to the impact on them of my serious illness so, lest the reader get the impression that I am at death's door, I should talk a bit about that. I have a predisposition to coronary artery disease; both my grandfathers died very young from heart attacks, and my father had his first coronary episode when he was sixty. Over the past twenty-eight years I have had a series of blockages in my coronary arteries but, thanks to the wonders of modern medicine, they have all been successfully treated with angioplasties, which took me out of commission for just two or three days. Fortunately, I have avoided a heart attack or bypass surgery.

About eight years ago, I woke up in the middle of the night with a terrible pain in my gut that turned out to be a volvulus: a twist in the small intestine. This led to complications with severe bleeding, hospitalization for several weeks, many transfusions of blood, two surgeries, and a prolonged convalescence. While I have made a full recovery, and, so far, suffer no after-effects, it was a grueling ordeal for me, even more for my wife, and set loose a variety of emotions in many of my long-term patients. Christine, Ann, and Yael all make reference to the impact of my life-threatening illness, and it brought out strong reactions in others.

While we had been considering retirement and a move to Northern California, the illness speeded up that decision and I told all my patients that I would be closing my practice in six months. For the first year and a half after the move north, I traveled to Los Angeles once a month for sessions with those patients who wished to have them. This eased the transition from intensive live contact to phone sessions or termination. A few patients were near the end of our work and took my move as an opportunity to finish. Others were referred to colleagues to continue their therapy. And a few, such as Rory, Yael, Nate, and Ann decided to continue with me by telephone or Skype. They did not feel they were ready to stop and our relationship had developed over such a long period that switching to someone else didn't feel right. Since we had become close over many years, we easily continued the therapy at a distance. And the fact that so many patients responded to my questionnaire is another indication of the long-lasting strength of our bond. So I am now retired—but not fully retired—with a small telephone practice and a continued involvement with writing.

11

Summing Up

Therapy is a wonderful, flawed, limited, potentially limitless process like life itself. None of us lives an ideal existence and none of us becomes "cured." But it gives us wonderful tools to glimpse beneath the surface layer of our existence, to pause, to check ourselves, to understand our behavior, to grow from the insight and experience—and repeat them all again, hopefully with more understanding.

—Leo

Josef Breuer, with his patient Bertha Pappenheim, invented "the talking cure," which was later modified and expanded by Freud into psychoanalysis. Breuer anticipated a modern relational approach by giving Bertha credit for naming the new methods that they worked out together. Nevertheless, Breuer and Freud were medical doctors and originally thought they were "curing" the sick patient's illness, "hysteria," and symptoms. As psychoanalysis evolved over the years, this medical model gradually faded; Freud even wrote an essay in 1926 arguing that medical training was not necessary for the practice of psychoanalysis.[1] While a number of my patients came to therapy with painful symptoms—anxiety states, depression, excessive guilt, eating disorders, obsessions, compulsions, and somatic complaints of various kinds—one of the most striking findings of their posttherapy responses is how little these are mentioned. Even Bernie, who came specifically because of panic attacks, does not mention these in his later account of the help he received from therapy. It is true that, for most of the patients, such symptoms were ameliorated or greatly diminished. But they don't focus on this, rather speaking of the complex changes in their personalities and relationship patterns. Again and again, they refer to greater feelings of self-acceptance, how hating themselves or feeling inadequate or inferior were replaced by greater confidence, higher self-esteem, the ability to assert themselves, growth in creativity, and a sense of mastery and competence.

119

A number of patients also experienced a reorganization in the way they understood the story of their lives: its meaning was perceived very differently.[2] In addition, many of them referred to increased access to their emotions, which made their lives richer and less constricted. In the words of Marie, "You told me that feelings are fact, a further validation that empowered me;" or as Leo put it, "Good therapy is like acting—when you need to, you can access the feeling more easily than other people, and it is in that catharsis, that the healing can happen." And, there were crucial changes in their relationship patterns, which led, for example, to leaving abusive or disappointing marriages and finding more satisfactory partners.

Emily made a more general point:

> *I think the two most important aspects of therapy are being present-listening and non-judgmentalism. When one is in therapy, those are the gifts your therapist gives to you. If you are paying attention to the process and you grow and get well from it, those are the gifts you give others for the rest of your life.*

Needless to say, such complex changes are dependent on the gradual growth of the relationship with the therapist and takes considerable time.

All these patients had the courage to persevere with their therapy even when it aroused disruptive emotions, cost money, took up significant time, opened up painful conflicts they were not aware of, and led to the disruption of familiar relationships. Their accounts of these psychological journeys are remarkably free of jargon, theory, and even my interpretations. The patients speak in their own voices, with insight, humor, and compassion for themselves and others. For some, writing these accounts led to further self-analysis, indicating that psychotherapy doesn't end when formal sessions stop but can be a life-long process of self-examination.

When I began this survey, I wasn't sure whether and how my former patients would respond. After many years in practice, I had a sense that I had become a fairly effective psychotherapist and that a number of them had benefited from our work together. At the time the therapy ended, some of them were no doubt still feeling their positive transference to me, which could have thrown a rosy glow over their assessments of the therapy. This should have dissipated over the years so that their responses many years later would give a more realistic and complete picture. Taken together, the accounts of these patients demonstrate the long lasting and deep personality changes that modern analytic psychotherapy can effect. Even so, I was not completely prepared for the gratitude that so many of them expressed. Looking back, with the help of these patient reports, I take a great deal of satisfaction in knowing that a large number of my patients were helped in deep and lasting ways. It has been my good fortune to be able to work for so long at something that was meaningful to others and that I really enjoyed.

Acknowledgments

Once again, I express my love and appreciation to my wife Barbara—first reader and perceptive critic—who created the title, and made significant contributions in many other ways. My thanks to my agent and friend John W. Wright for his support and continuing faith in my work. Several friends and colleagues took time from their busy schedules to read early versions of the book and offer helpful suggestions. These include: George Atwood, Joseph Barber, Philip Bromberg, Bob Carrere, Suzanne Gassner, Christopher Gelber, Dave Markel, Tom Rosbrow, Jeffrey Rubin, Jon Seirup, Phillip Shaver, and Judith Viorst. My thanks to all of you. Finally, my deepest appreciation to all the patients whose accounts of their psychotherapy make up the heart of this book.

Notes

Prologue

1. *Accept this "wisdom":* The major new approaches that make up contemporary psychoanalysis were preceded by the work of the Neo-Freudians. For accounts of their ideas, see Paris (1994) on Karen Horney; Erik Erikson (1950); Mauricio Cortina and Michael Maccoby (1996) on Erich Fromm; and Harry Stack Sullivan (1953). For accounts of the relational and interpersonal schools, originally derived from Sullivan's work, see Lewis Aron (1996), Philip Bromberg (1998 and 2006), and Stephen Mitchell (1988). For self-psychology, see Heinz Kohut (1977). For the intersubjective approach, see Robert Stolorow, Bernard Brandschaft, and George Atwood (1987). For the control-mastery method, see Joseph Weiss (1993) and George Silberschatz (2005). For attachment theory, see John Bowlby (1969, 1973, and 1980), Cassidy and Shaver (2010), and Mikulinca and Shaver (2010). Peter Rudnytsky (2003) presents an excellent discussion of a number of these theories.

2. *About themselves:* One exception that I am aware of is Stuart Perlman who, in his 1999 book, relates his own traumatic history to his work with traumatized patients.

Chapter 1

1. *Orthodox doctrines:* Freud was the first to establish psychoanalysis as an orthodoxy with its own terminology, treatment methods, and dogmas. Even as they broke away from him and his "movement," others, such as Jung and Adler, followed the pattern of establishing a "school" led by a charismatic leader, a trend that has continued to the present. Thus, there are "Jungians," "Adlerians," "Kleinians," and, now, "Kohutians." As Paul Stepansky points out in *Psychoanalysis at the Margins* (2009), despite talk of "theoretical pluralism," contemporary schools of psychoanalysis are still encapsulated in-groups—not much influenced by each other—that rarely communicate or share ideas. For an in-depth look at what actually goes on in American psychoanalytic institutes, see Kirsner's *Unfree Associations: Inside Psychoanalytic Institutes* (2009). A special problem of psychoanalytic training comes from the transferences that develop between candidates and their training analysts, who are typically senior members. Training analyses are often exploited for political purposes, producing younger analysts who do not feel free to express views at odds with their former analysts (see Kirsner 2010).

2. *Spirituality and religions*: I have seen at least two patients—not included in this book—who were deeply involved in religion. One was a Christian minister and the other a graduate student, very committed to his church. Although these patients knew I did not share their religious views, this did not seem to create any problems in therapy. In my view, the best book integrating spirituality and contemporary analytic therapy is that by my friend and colleague, the late Randy Sorenson, *Minding Spirituality* (2004).

3. *Buddhism*: an excellent book that reviews Buddhist practice and brings it together with psychotherapy is Jeffrey Rubin's *Psychotherapy and Buddhism: Toward an Integration* (1996). See also Rubin's *The Art of Flourishing* (2011).

4. *Rules and techniques*: Psychoanalysis, from Freud to the present, has been top-heavy with theory, which takes therapists away from the methods—attentive listening, empathy, warmth, friendliness, interpretations that fit the individual—that are at the heart of effective treatment. In fact, a preoccupation with complex theory and jargon may create emotional distance between therapist and patient. Stepansky (2009) has a valuable discussion of this issue and, for a withering critique, see Nathan Leites' *The New Ego* (1971).

5. *Freud had counseled*: Freud's recommendations on psychoanalytic technique are contained in five papers (Freud 1911, 1912a, 1912b, 1913, 1914a, and 1914b).

6. *My experience*: The kind of analytic therapy I practice is similar to that described in the writings of many contemporary workers. In researching the literature I came upon a number of therapists who advocate an approach quite similar to mine. This literature provides evidence for the effectiveness of relational factors, including: empathy, friendliness, expressions of care, warmth, support, openness, activity, and helping patients discover things about themselves they were not aware of. Shedler (2010, 2011) presents an excellent review of a very large number of studies that demonstrate the effectiveness of what he terms "psychodynamic psychotherapy." As he puts it,

> *Effect sizes for psychodynamic therapy are as large as those reported for other therapies that have been actively promoted as "empirically supported" and "evidence based." In addition, patients who receive psychodynamic therapy maintain therapeutic gains and appear to continue to improve after treatment ends. Finally, nonpsychodynamic therapies may be effective in part because the more skilled practitioners utilize techniques that have long been central to psychodynamic theory and practice. The perception that psychodynamic approaches lack empirical support does not accord with available scientific evidence and may reflect selective dissemination of research findings.* (Shedler 2010, 98)

Studies that give further support to Shedler's overall assessment include: Bush (forthcoming); Curtis et al. (2004); Holmes (1998); Lerchenring and Rabung (2008); and Schachter and Kachele (2007). Norcross' 2002 book provides a comprehensive review of a great deal of research that demonstrates the effective factors in psychotherapy. Rebecca Curtis' *Desire, Self, Mind, and the Psychotherapies* (2009) provides a comprehensive discussion of a very broad and open approach to psychotherapy and related forms of treatment.

7. *Long-term follow-up*: While I did not have it in mind when I began this project, the responses of my patients constitute a very long-term follow-up of the effects of analytic psychotherapy. Some of them were seen twenty and thirty years before responding to my questionnaire. Most of the follow-ups in psychotherapy research are six months or, at the most, one year, though there are a very small number that go beyond this limit. More recent longer-term follow-up studies of CBT indicate that the results do not hold up so well over time (see Durham et al. 2005; Nadiga et al. 2003; and Paykel et al. 2005). To see how the therapy described here affected the patients' lives many years later is unique in the field. A problem with relying on such a long period of time between the end of their therapy and their response to my questionnaire may be that other events could have occurred to account for the changes the patients describe. Also, some conditions, such as cyclical depressions, remit without outside interventions. Readers will have to make up their own minds as to whether the things the patients describe can be attributed to their therapy. A number of them think that the changes in their lives were strongly affected by their treatments. My own sense is that the complex personality problems that changed are not the kind of things that "spontaneously remit" without psychotherapeutic intervention.

A related point concerns the length of a number of these therapies, which range from a few years to, in one case, thirty-five years. The crucial point is whether change has occurred over these long periods. I think it has. Several of the cases in Chapter 4 illustrate the contrast between old and contemporary forms of analytic therapy and, as should be clear, length of the treatment is not the important difference.

Chapter 2

1. *Nor was she*: I referred Scott's wife to a colleague who she saw for a few sessions. His sense was that she was a far more disturbed woman than I imagined: very isolated and extremely limited in the few relationships she did have.

2. *Self starvation*: on at least two occasions, Gregor hit family members when they were in restaurants.

Chapter 4

1. *Height of his powers*: The account of Hirst's treatment—which Freud himself never publicly reported—can be found in Lynn (1997). Kardiner's 1977 *Reminiscences* contains most of the information about the other cases. See also my 2000 biography of Freud, especially pages 185–8, and 277–9.

2. *Penis in his breast*: These Kleinian interpretations always bring to mind Lenny Bruce's autobiography, *How to Talk Dirty and Influence People* (1965). The jargon makes the therapist feel like he or she is dealing with "deep" and "primitive" material while, in my view, this kind of talk is a way of keeping distance from the patient's actual emotional life. For a good—or bad—example, see Mason (1987).

3. *For my life*: Nino's first two experiences in therapy show how a focus on theory-derived interpretations or the transference led his analysts to miss the importance of something obvious: the loss of his first love. Another example is provided by the therapists who saw Lark's husband Howard, whose anorexia/bulimia was so severe that it was almost impossible to miss, yet it was never even mentioned, much less dealt with, in over ten years of classical psychoanalysis.

4. *Analysts were doing*: an important discussion of this "pathological accommodation" can be found in Brandchaft (2007). Patients who have been abused—sexually, physically, or emotionally—as children are commonly lied to about these experiences by their abusers or threatened with further harm if they tell anyone what they have undergone. Thus, they are very cautious about revealing the abuse to their therapists. This is probably why analysts who don't believe in the importance of such experiences—who trace such reports to the child's instincts or fantasies—rarely hear reports of abuse. The patients sense they will, once again, not be believed, and don't reveal what has happened to them. For a very moving account of the treatment of a severely traumatized woman, and the toll it can take on the therapist, see Perlmen (2009). Atwood (2011) describes a number of such cases.

5. *In later life*: an excellent source reviewing the effects of adult onset trauma is Ghislaine Boulanger's book, *Wounded by Reality* (2007).

Chapter 5

1. *Admitted to Cornell*: If the reader is wondering how I managed to go to a relatively expensive Ivy League college when my family had so little money, I should explain that I worked and saved all the year before, and got a job in the cafeteria at Cornell to make ends meet, which they never quite did. As an active eighteen-year-old, I was always a little hungry. My meager funds, along with the freezing winter—hard on a boy raised in Los Angeles—led me to leave after one year.

Chapter 6

1. *Bowlby's work*: John Bowlby began publishing articles on what would eventually become attachment theory in the late 1950s. Detailed accounts can be found in Bowlby (1969, 1973, and 1980). Work on attachment, separation, and loss has been carried forth by Mary Ainsworth and many other co-workers and later researchers, including those doing observations of mother–infant interactions, as well as the development of the Adult Attachment Interview. As just one of these other projects, see Main et al. (1985). See also Cassidy and Shaver (2010), and Mikulincer and Shaver (2010). Alan Sroufe and his colleagues (2005) have done an outstanding longitudinal study of personality development which demonstrates the multitude of experiences that shape the person from birth to adulthood. Still, while they note the importance of a great many factors, type of attachment emerged as the single-most influential one.

2. *Sympathetic to Rogers*: Carl Rogers inspired a group of students and colleagues to do research on therapy, or what he called "counseling." The major

factors that they identified as leading to successful outcomes are remarkably consistent with recent research findings on what works in contemporary analytic psychotherapy as well as what emerges from the responses of my patients: "unconditional positive regard," "accurate empathy," "non-possessive warmth," and "congruence."

3. *Other investigators*: Research and theory on dreaming that is consistent with our findings can be found in the work of Ray Greenberg and his colleagues (1975, 1978), as well as in the work of Walter Bonime (1962), Thomas French and Erika Fromm (1964), and Charles Rycroft (1979).

4. *Not restricted to sexuality*: recent research on REM sleep in the laboratory of Matt Walker gives support to the ideas about the function of dreams outlined in my 1967 paper (see Walker 2009).

5. *Theories of motivation*: I was invited by the psychoanalyst Judd Marmor to contribute a chapter, critical of psychoanalytic drive theory, to a book he was editing titled *Modern Psychoanalysis* (Breger 1968). There, I drew on the work of Robert R. Holt (1989), George S. Klein (1976), Jane Loevinger (1976), and others.

6. *Sessions or less*: This work was influenced by David Malan's 1976 book on brief psychotherapy (see Levene, Breger, and Patterson 1972).

7. *On their heads*: Bischof presents a convincing case that all animal species have a biologically built-in tendency to avoid reproduction with members of their own families. In humans, this does not become apparent until adolescence, but all cultures have customs that promote marriage outside the primary group. The main reason for this biological imperative is that in-breeding increases the likelihood of genetic defects while out-breeding promotes hybrid vigor. Thus, Freud's belief that humans have to fight against incestuous instincts is bad biology, and was known to be so during his lifetime.

Chapter 7

1. *What was useful*: A wonderful satirical account of psychoanalytic training can be found in Samuel Shem's novel, *Mount Misery* (1997).

2. *Need of sublimation*: Masters and Johnson (1966) demonstrated by empirical research that clitoral stimulation was necessary for female orgasm but their findings, falling outside of the orthodox fold, were ignored by psychoanalysts who continued to cling to Freud's unsubstantiated ideas. Maines (1999) presents a fascinating account of the hidden history of the vibrator. She shows that many physicians—not to mention women themselves—have been aware for centuries that sexual intercourse that consists solely of the stimulation provided by penile penetration frequently leaves the woman unsatisfied, without orgasm. Freud's theory had things backward; it is not that vaginal orgasms are normal but that stimulation of the clitoris is frequently necessary for a woman's satisfaction.

3. *No great Oedipal*: Not one of the thirty-one patients described in this book suffered from an "Oedipus complex" of the kind Freud believed was at the core of everyone's neurosis. See Friedman and Downey (2002) for a comprehensive critical discussion of the Oedipus complex.

4. *Theories of Heinz Kohut*: Kohut has inspired the school of contemporary psychoanalysis known as self-psychology with a series of articles and books (Kohut 1977 provides a clear account). Self-psychology has developed into a major movement—with offshoots and factions—publications by a number of other authors, journals, and conferences.

5. *And Langley Porter*: When I became director of the training clinic at the University of Oregon, I made the graduate students coparticipants in its functioning. At Langley Porter, our setting up the brief psychotherapy program was a clear break from the medical–diagnostic approach that outpatients had previously been subjected to. I also pushed to have the staff take over our weekly meetings and elect our own chairperson.

6. *Analysis with him*: For the biographies, I drew on the work of a number of writers, including the Neo-Freudians and many contemporary psychoanalysts. Also valuable was new research and evidence, such as Freud's complete letters to Wilhelm Fliess—we all owe Jeffrey Masson a great debt for making these public (see Masson 1985)—as well as the correspondence with C. G. Jung, Sandor Ferenczi, Ernest Jones, and others. Then there were the invaluable accounts by five patients who were in psychoanalysis with Freud and wrote about their experience: Smiley Blanton (1971), John Dorsey (1976), the poet H. D.—Hilda Doolittle—(1956), Abram Kardiner (1977), and Joseph Wortis (1954). Additional descriptions of Freud's cases can be found in Roazen (1975), and in interviews with former patients in Roazen (1995).

Chapter 8

1. *Corrective emotional experience*: This is a concept developed by Franz Alexander, along with his collaborator Thomas French (see Alexander and French 1946). Alexander had earlier done pioneering work on psychosomatic medicine and brief psychotherapy. The idea of a "corrective emotional experience" was that the analyst provides the patient with those emotional-relational experiences that he or she missed out on in childhood. It was the opposite of the classical psychoanalytic techniques of deprivation and abstinence, and anticipated contemporary forms of analytic therapy. As was typical, Alexander was attacked by classical Freudians and his methods labeled heretical.

2. *Small head*: One of Nate's disturbing symptoms when he began therapy was an obsessive belief that his head was too small, which led him to continually check his reflection to make sure this wasn't so. In fact, he was a good-looking young man, of normal size for his age. I made no attempt to interpret the meaning of this belief—that it symbolized his feeling small, without an identity, lost in a nightmare—and it gradually passed.

3. *All other interpretations*: For a critical discussion of the overemphasis on transference interpretations and other Freudian shibboleths, see Curtis (2009).

Chapter 9

1. *Visited him...in the hospital*: I know a man whose psychoanalyst visited him in the hospital after a serous illness and then decided that he couldn't

see him in analysis anymore because the "neutrality" had been breached. Just at the time when this young person was most vulnerable, his analyst dropped him because the classical rules required him to.

2. *Borderline personality disorder*: A good description and review of this condition, along with many useful references, can be found on the Wikipedia site for "borderline personality disorder."

Chapter 11

1. *Practice psychoanalysis*: Whether psychoanalysis is a branch of medicine or not has been a vexed issue. In America, in order to gain legitimacy and prestige, organized psychoanalysis aligned itself with medicine and restricted training to psychiatrists, though this is no longer true. But vestiges of the old affiliation with medicine hung on for many years, with talk of diagnostic categories such as "hysteria," "obsessive-compulsive neurosis," and the like, though a careful examination of actual cases—including Freud's own—provided little support for these views. Psychiatrist-psychoanalysts—until fairly recently—continued some of this medical sounding talk, though it was clear that what they actually practiced was an interpersonal, interpretive endeavor. See Wallerstein (1998).

2. *Perceived very differently*: In *Acts of Meaning* (1990), Jerome Bruner presents a very insightful discussion of the ways lives are defined by the meanings individuals assign to them. Human beings create narratives that make sense of the events that constitute their lives. One way to look at the changes my patients experienced in their therapy is as a reorganization of their life narratives.

Bibliography

Ablon, J. S., and E. E. Jones. "How Expert Clinicians' Prototypes of an Ideal Treatment Correlate with Outcome in Psychodynamic and Cognitive-Behavioral Therapy." *Psychotherapy Research* 8 (1998): 71–83.

Alexander, F., T. M. French et al. *Psychoanalytic Therapy: Principles and Applications.* New York, NY: Ronald Press, 1946.

Angell, M. "The Epidemic of Mental Illness: Why?" *The New York Review of Books* (June 23, 2011): 20–22.

_____. "The Illusions of Psychiatry, Part II." *The New York Review of Books* (July 14, 2011): 20–22.

Aron, L. *A Meeting of Minds: Mutuality in Psychoanalysis.* Hillsdale, NJ: The Analytic Press, 1996.

Atwood, G. E. *The Abyss of Madness: Clinical Explorations.* New York, NY: Routledge, 2011.

Blanton, S. *Diary of My Analysis with Sigmund Freud.* New York, NY: Hawthorn Books, 1971.

Bonime, W. *The Clinical Use of Dreams.* New York, NY: Basic Books, 1962.

Bowlby, J. *Attachment and Loss. Vol. 1: Attachment.* New York, NY: Basic Books, 1969.

_____. *Attachment and Loss. Vol. 2: Separation.* New York, NY: Basic Books, 1973.

_____. *Attachment and Loss. Vol. 3: Loss, Sadness and Depression.* New York, NY: Basic Books, 1980.

Brandchaft, B. "Systems of Pathological Accommodation and Change in Analysis." *Psychoanalytic Psychology* 24 (2007): 667–87.

Breger, L. *Dostoevsky: The Author as Psychoanalyst.* New York, NY: New York University Press, 1989. Reissued by Transaction Publishers, 2009.

_____. *A Dream of Undying Fame: How Freud Betrayed His Mentor and Invented Psychoanalysis.* New York, NY: Basic Books, 2009.

_____. *The Effect of Stress on Dreams* (with Ian Hunter and Ron W. Lane.). New York, NY: *Psychological Issues*, No. 27, 1971.

_____. *Freud: Darkness in the Midst of Vision.* New York, NY: John Wiley, 2000.

_____. *Freud's Unfinished Journey: Conventional and Critical Perspectives in Psychoanalytic Theory.* London, Boston, and Henley: Routledge & Kegan Paul, 1981.

_____. *From Instinct to Identity: The Development of Personality.* Englewood Cliffs, NJ: Prentice Hall, 1974. Reissued by Transaction Publishers, 2009.

_____. "Function of Dreams." *Journal of Abnormal Psychology Monograph* 72 (1967): 1–28.

_____. "The Manifest Dream and Its Latent Meaning." In *The Dream in Clinical Practice.* Edited by J. Natterson, 3–27. New York, NY: Jason Aronson, 1980.

_____. "Motivation, Energy, and Cognitive Structure in Psychoanalytic Theory." In *Modern Psychoanalysis: New Directions and Perspectives.* Edited by J. Marmor, 44–65. New York, NY: Basic Books, 1968.

_____. "Some Metaphorical Types Met with in Psychoanalytic Theory." *Psychoanalysis and Contemporary Thought* 4 (1981): 107–40.

Breger, L., and J. L. McGaugh, "Critique and Reformulation of 'Learning Theory' Approaches to Psychotherapy and Neurosis." *Psychological Bulletin* 63 (1965): 338–58.

Bromberg, P. M. *Awakening the Dreamer in the Dream.* Mahwah, NJ: The Analytic Press, 2006.

_____. *Standing in the Spaces: Essays on Clinical Process, Trauma and Dissociation.* Hillsdale, NJ: The Analytic Press, 1998.

Bruce, L. *How to Talk Dirty and Influence People.* Chicago, IL: Playboy Press, 1965.

Bruner, J. *Acts of Meaning.* Cambridge, MA: Harvard University Press, 1990.

Bush, M. "Should Supportive Measures and Relational Variables be Considered a Part of Psychoanalytic Technique? Some Empirical Considerations." *International Journal of Psychoanalysis* (Forthcoming).

Carlat, D. *Unhinged: The Trouble with Psychiatry—A Doctor's Revelations about a Profession in Crisis.* New York, NY: The Free Press, 2010.

Cassidy, J., and P. R. Shaver, eds. *Handbook of Attachment Theory and Research.* New York, NY: Guilford Press, 1999.

Cortina, M., and M. Maccoby, eds. *A Prophetic Analyst: Erich Fromm's Contributions to Psychoanalysis.* Northvale, NJ: Jason Aronson, 1996.

Curtis, R. C. *Desire, Self, Mind and the Psychotherapies: Unifying Science and Psychoanalysis.* Lanham, MD: Jason Aronson, 2008.

Curtis, R., C. Field, I. Knaan-Kostman, and K. Mannix, "What 75 Psychoanalysts Found Helpful and Hurtful in Their Own Analysis." *Psychoanalytic Psychology* 21 (2004): 183–202.

Dorsey, J. M. *An American Psychiatrist in Vienna: 1935-1937, and His Sigmund Freud.* Detroit, MI: Center for Health Education, 1976.

Durham, R. C. et al. "Long-term Outcome of Cognitive Behaviour Therapy Clinical Trials in Central Scotland." *Health Technology Assessment* 9 (2005): 1–174.

French, T. M., and E. Fromm. *Dream Interpretation: A New Approach.* New York, NY: Basic Books, 1964.

All the following titles are from *The Standard Edition of the Complete Psychological Works of Sigmund Freud,* edited and translated by James Strachey, in collaboration with Anna Freud, assisted by Alix Strachey and Alan Tyson. London: Hogarth Press. Works are cited by title, volume, date, and page number.

Freud, S. *Analysis Terminable and Interminable,* 23, 1937, 211–53.

_____. *The Dynamics of the Transference,* 12, 1912a, 97–108.

_____. *The Handling of Dream-Interpretation in Psychoanalysis,* 12, 1911, 85–96.

_____. *The Interpretation of Dreams,* 4 and 5, 1900, 1–627.

_____. *"Introduction" to Psycho-Analysis and the War Neuroses,* 17, 1919, 206–10.

_____. *Observations on Transference-Love (Further Recommendations on the Technique of Psycho-Analysis III),* 12, 1914b, 157–71.

_____. *On Beginning the Treatment (Further Recommendations on the Technique of Psycho-Analysis, I),* 12, 1913, 121–44.

_____. *Psychoanalytic Notes on an Autobiographical Account of a Case of Paranoia (Dementia Paranoids),* 12, 1911, 3–82.

_____. *The Question of Lay Analysis,* 20, 1926, 179–258.

_____. *Recommendations to Physicians Practicing Psycho-Analysis,* 12, 1912b, 109–20.

_____. *Remembering, Repeating and Working-Through (Further Recommendations on the Technique of Psychoanalysis II),* 12, 1914a, 145–56.

Friedman, R. C., and J. I. Downey. *Sexual Orientation and Psychoanalysis: Sexual Science and Clinical Practice.* New York, NY: Columbia University Press, 2002.

Gabriel, R. A. *No More Heroes: Madness and Psychiatry in War.* New York, NY: Hill & Wang, 1987.

Greenberg, R. "A Psychoanalytic Dream Continuum: The Source and Function of Dreams." *International Review of Psychoanalysis* 2 (1975): 441–48.

_____. "If Freud Only Knew: A Reconsideration of Psychoanalytic Dream Theory." *International Review of Psychoanalysis* 5 (1978): 71–75.

H. D. (Hilda Doolittle). *Tribute to Freud.* New York, NY: New Directions, 1956.

Holmes, J. "The Changing Aims of Psychoanalytic Psychotherapy: An Integrative Perspective." *International Journal of Psycho-Analysis* 79 (1998): 227–40.

Holt, R. R. *Freud Reappraised: A Fresh Look at Psychoanalytic Theory.* New York, NY: Guilford Press, 1989.

Kardiner, A. *My Analysis with Freud: Reminiscences.* New York, NY: W. W. Norton, 1977.

Kirsch, I. *The Emperor's New Drugs: Exploding the Antidepressant Myth.* New York, NY: Basic Books, 2011.

Kirsner, D. "Training Analysis: The Shibboleth of Psychoanalytic Education." *Psychoanalytic Review* 97 (2010): 971–95.

_____. *Unfree Associations: Inside Psychoanalytic Institutes.* Updated ed. Lanham, MD: Jason Aronson, 2009.

Klein, G. S. *Psychoanalytic Theory: An Exploration of Essentials.* New York, NY: International Universities Press, 1976.

Kohut, H. *The Restoration of the Self.* New York, NY: International Universities Press, 1977.

Leichsenring, F., and S. Rabung. "Effectiveness of Long-term Psychodynamic Psychotherapy: A Meta-analysis." *Journal of the American Medical Association* 300 (2008): 1551–65.

Leites, N. *The New Ego: Pitfalls in Current Thinking about Patients in Psychoanalysis.* Santa Rosa, CA: Science House, 1971.

Levene, H. A., L. Breger, and V. Patterson. "A Training and Research Program in Brief Psychotherapy." *American Journal of Psychotherapy* 26 (1972): 90–100.

Lieberman, E. J. *Acts of Will: The Life and Work of Otto Rank.* New York, NY: The Free Press, 1985.

Lifton, R. J. *Home from the War: Learning from Vietnam Veterans.* Boston, MA: Beacon Press. 1973.

Loevinger, J. *Ego Development.* San Francisco, CA: Jossey-Bass, 1976.

Lynn, D. J., and G. E. Vaillant. "Anonymity, Neutrality, and Confidentiality in the Actual Methods of Sigmund Freud: A Review of Forty-three Cases, 1907-1939." *American Journal of Psychiatry* 155, no. 2 (1998): 163–71.

Main, M., N. Kaplan, and J. Cassidy. "Security in Infancy, Childhood and Adulthood: A Move to the Level of Representation." *Monographs of the Society for Research in Child Development* 50 (1–2, Serial No. 209) (1985): 66–104.

Maines, R. P. *The Technology of Orgasm: 'Hysteria,' the Vibrator, and Woman's Sexual Satisfaction.* Baltimore, MD: Johns Hopkins University Press, 1999.

Malan, D. H. *The Frontiers of Brief Psychotherapy.* New York, NY: Plenum Press, 1976.

Maroda, K. *The Power of Countertransference.* 2nd ed. New York, NY: Routledge, 2004.

_____. *Seduction, Surrender, and Transformation: Emotional Engagement in the Analytic Process.* Hillsdale, NJ: The Analytic Press, 1999.

Mason, A. "A Kleinian Perspective." *Psychoanalytic Inquiry* 7, no. 2 (1987): 189–97.

Masson, J. M., ed. and trans. *The Complete Letters of Sigmund Freud to Wilhelm Fliess: 1887-1904*. Cambridge, MA: Harvard University Press, 1985.

_____. *Final Analysis: The Making and Unmaking of a Psychoanalyst*. New York, NY: Fontana, 1992.

Masters, W. H., and V. F. Johnson. *Human Sexual Response*. Boston, MA: Little, Brown, 1966.

McGuire, W., ed. *The Freud/Jung Letters: The Correspondence between Sigmund Freud and C. G. Jung*. Translated by R. Manheim and R. F. C. Hull. Princeton, NJ: Princeton University Press, 1974.

Mikulincer, M., and P. R. Shaver. *Attachment in Adulthood: Structure, Dynamics and Change*. New York, NY: Guilford Press, 2010.

Mitchell, S. A. *Relational Concepts in Psychoanalysis*. Cambridge, MA: Harvard University Press, 1988.

Nadiga, D. N. et al. "Review of Long-term Effectiveness of Cognitive Behavioural Therapy Compared to Medication in Panic Disorder." *Depression and Anxiety* 17 (2003): 58–64.

Norcross, J. C. *Psychotherapy: Relationships That Work*. New York, NY: Oxford University Press, 2002.

Paris, B. J. *Karen Horney: A Psychoanalyst's Search for Self-understanding*. New Haven, CT and London: Yale University Press, 1994.

Paykel, E. S. et al. "Cognitive Behavioural Therapy Has Short Term But Not Long Term Benefits in People with Residual Symptoms of Depression." *Psychological Medicine* 35 (2005): 59–68.

Perlman, S. D. "I Do This for Your Own Good: A Story of Shrieking, Disaster and Recovery." *The American Journal of Psychoanalysis* 69 (2009): 330–47.

_____. *The Therapists Emotional Survival: Dealing with the Pain of Exploring Trauma*. Northvale, NJ: Jason Aronson, 1999.

Roazen, P. *Freud and His Followers*. New York, NY: Knopf, 1975.

_____. *How Freud Worked: First-Hand Accounts of Patients*. Northvale, NJ: Jason Aronson, 1995.

Ross, J. M. "Psychoanalysis, the Anxiety of Influence, and the Sadomasochism of Everyday Life." *Journal of Applied Psychoanalysis* 1 (1999): 57–78.

Roth, A., and P. Fonagy. *What Works for Whom? A Critical Review of Psychotherapy Research*. New York and London: Guilford Press, 1996.

Rubin, J. B. *The Art of Flourishing*. New York, NY: Crown Archetype, 2011.

_____. *Psychotherapy and Buddhism: Toward an Integration*. New York and London: Plenum Press, 1996.

Rudnytsky, P. *Reading Psychoanalysis: Freud, Rank, Ferenczi and Groddeck*. Ithaca, NY: Cornell University Press, 2003.

Rycroft, C. *The Innocence of Dreams*. New York, NY: Pantheon, 1979.

Schachter, J., ed. *Transforming Lives: Analyst and Patient View the Power of Psychoanalytic Treatment*. Lanham, MD: Jason Aronson, 2005.

Schachter, J., and H. Kachele. "The Analyst's Role in Healing: Psychoanalysis-plus." *Psychoanalytic Psychology* 24 (2007): 429–44.

Shedler, J. "The Efficacy of Psychodynamic Psychotherapy." *American Psychologist* 65 (2010): 98–109.

_____. "Science or Ideology? Reply to Comments." *American Psychologist* 66 (2011): 152–54.

Shem, S. *Mount Misery*. New York, NY: Fawcett, 1997.

Silberschatz, G., ed. *Transformative Relationships: The Control Mastery Theory of Psychotherapy*. New York and Hove: Routledge, 2005.

Slade, A. "The Implications of Attachment Theory and Research for Adult Psychotherapy: Research and Clinical Perspectives." In *Handbook of Attachment Theory and Research*. Edited by J. Cassidy and P. Shaver, 575–95. New York, NY: Guilford Press, 1999.

Sorenson, R. L. *Minding Spirituality*. Hillsdale NJ: The Analytic Press, 2004.

Sroufe, L. A., B. Egeland, E. A. Carlson, and W. A. Collins. *The Development of the Person: The Minnesota Study of Risk and Adaptation from Birth to Adulthood*. New York, NY: Guilford Press, 2005.

Stepansky, P. E. *Psychoanalysis at the Margins*. New York, NY: Other Press, 2009.

Stoller, R. J. *Splitting: A Case of Female Masculinity*. Chicago, IL: Quadrangle, 1973.

Stolorow, R. D., B. Brandchaft, and G. E. Atwood. *Psychoanalytic Treatment: An Intersubjective Approach*. Hillsdale, NJ: Analytic Press, 1987.

Strupp, H. H. "Some Salient Lessons from Research and Practice." *Psychotherapy* 33 (1996): 135–38.

Sullivan, H. S. *The Interpersonal Theory of Psychiatry*. New York and London: W. W. Norton, 1953.

Summers, R. F., and J. P. Barber. *Psychodynamic Therapy: A Guide to Evidence-based Practice*. New York, NY: Guilford Press, 2010.

Trillin, C. *Remembering Denny*. New York, NY: Farrar, Straus & Giroux, 1993.

Turner, E. H. et al. "Selective Publication of Antidepressant Trials and Its Influence on Apparent Efficacy." *New England Journal of Medicine* 358 (2008): 252–60.

Wachtel, P. L. "On Theory, Practice, and the Nature of Integration." In *The Restoration of Dialogue: Readings in the Philosophy of Clinical Psychology*. Edited by R. B. Miller, 418–32. Washington, DC: American Psychological Association, 1992.

Walker, M. R. "The Role of Sleep in Cognition and Emotions." *New York Academy of Science* 1156 (2009): 168–97.

Wallerstein, R. S. *42 Lives in Treatment: A Study of Psychoanalysis and Psychotherapy*. New York, NY: Guilford Press, 1986.

_____. *Lay Analysis: Life Inside the Controversy*. Hillsdale, NJ: The Analytic Press, 1998.

Wampold, B. E. *The Great Psychotherapy Debate: Models, Methods and Findings*. New York, NY: Routledge, 2001.

Webster, B. *The Last Good Freudian*. New York and London: Holmes & Meier, 2000.

Weiss, J. *How Psychotherapy Works: Process and Technique*. New York, NY: Guilford Press, 1993.

Whitaker, R. *Anatomy of an Epidemic: Magic Bullets, Psychiatric Drugs, and the Astonishing Rise of Mental Illness in America*. New York, NY: Crown, 2010.

Wortis, J. *Fragments of an Analysis with Freud*. New York, NY: Simon & Schuster, 1954.

Yalom, I., and G. Elkin. *Every Day Gets a Little Closer: A Twice-told Therapy*. New York, NY: Basic Books, 1991.

Index